ORGANIZATIONAL
PATHOLOGY

ORGANIZATIONAL
PATHOLOGY
Life and Death of Organizations

Yitzhak Samuel

Transaction Publishers
New Brunswick (U.S.A.) and London (U.K.)

Copyright © 2010 by Transaction Publishers, New Brunswick, New Jersey.

All rights reserved under International and Pan-American Copyright Conventions. No part of this book may be reproduced or transmitted in any form or by any means, electronic or mechanical, including photocopy, recording, or any information storage and retrieval system, without prior permission in writing from the publisher. All inquiries should be addressed to Transaction Publishers, Rutgers—The State University of New Jersey, 35 Berrue Circle, Piscataway, New Jersey 08854-8042. www.transactionpub.com

This book is printed on acid-free paper that meets the American National Standard for Permanence of Paper for Printed Library Materials.
Library of Congress Catalog Number: 2009018814
ISBN: 978-1-4128-1064-7
Printed in the United States of America

Library of Congress Cataloging-in-Publication Data

Samuel, Yitzhak.
    Organizational pathology : life and death of organizations / Yitzhak Samuel.
        p. cm.
    Includes bibliographical references and index.
    ISBN 978-1-4128-1064-7
    1. Organizational effectiveness. I. Title.

HD58.9.S256 2009
302.3'5--dc22

                                    2009018814

To my beloved grandchildren, Gil and Tal Gutter.

Contents

Acknowledgements

It is my pleasure to express my gratitude to those who assisted me in various ways to complete and publish this volume. Primarily, I would like to thank my colleague and friend Stewart Clegg, at the University of Technology Sydney, for his encouragement and assistance. Stewart made it possible for me to spend my sabbatical at the UTS School of Management as a Visiting Scholar; there, I was able to get away from my academic and administrative duties and devote my time to the writing a great deal of this book.

My colleagues and friends: Jim Taylor, Micha Popper, Gideon Fishman, Arye Rattner, Arye Reshef, and Stewart Clegg, kindly previewed various parts of the manuscript and contributed useful comments and suggestions. Jim and Stewart also wrote complimenting reviews. I would like to thank The University of Haifa's Vice President and Dean of Research, Majid Al Haj; and the Chair of the Department of Sociology and Anthropology, Gustavo Mesch for their financial support.

My thanks are also due to Murray Rosovsky, Lee Cornfield, and Jennifer Nippins for their fine editorial work. My Research assistants, then, Yuval Holtzman and Einat Ivry helped greatly with library search.

Finally, I wish to acknowledge my beloved family: my wife Yael, my daughter Sigal, and my son in-law Amir, for their love, encouragement, advice, and support. My grandchildren, Gil and Tal, to whom I dedicate this book, have been an endless source of joy and pride to me.

Preface

For quite a long time, I have been interested in learning about the downfall and disappearance of organizations, its causes and consequences. This interest was both academic and practical. While I was serving as an organizational consultant for many years, I had the opportunity to diagnose and to take care of various organizational problems. As a sociologist by training, for me, the concept of "organizations" is much broader than the restricted focus on businesses alone. It refers also to political parties, labor unions, prisons, military and police forces, voluntary associations, and many others as well. Thus, I have been astonished to realize just how frequently organizations of all kinds everywhere disappear. In the past, as in the present, empires have dissolved and nation-states have disintegrated, not to mention the recent collapse of large banks and giant corporations.

A few years ago, I concluded that graduate students analyzing organizations ought to study the phenomenon of failure more broadly and deeply than they are required to do in most graduate programs. Hence, I prepared a graduate-level seminar on that subject matter, which I taught for several academic years. My teaching experience during those years was enlightening for me as well, as I noticed that my students were very interested in this unusual seminar and actively participated in class. That experience enabled me to better define this agenda of study and to concentrate on its major issues.

Thus, both my academic and practical experiences taught me that most organizations collapsed due to their own deficiencies, which in turn made it difficult for them to cope effectively with severe pressures, whether these came from within or from outside sources. Following that insight, I looked for an appropriate concept that might serve as a sort of an umbrella term, under which a variety of causes and consequences of organizations' failure could be grouped together. Incidentally, I have noticed that whenever an organization falls into a serious trouble, some observers react by saying something along these lines: "Well, this is a really sick organization and it will [should] not survive anyway."

In light of these and other considerations, I have chosen the term "organizational pathology" to serve as an appropriate reference to the various causes and consequences of such downfalls. Moreover, the term "pathology" is not merely a tag name in this context; although it serves as a metaphor, it also represents a certain perspective on the life and death of organizations and provides a framework that guides the present volume. To the best of my knowledge, this is probably the first professional book devoted to the idea of organizational pathology.

This volume addresses the various ways in which organizations reach their end. It discusses variables that are responsible for organizations' failure and death. One chapter analyzes various illnesses and disorders that affect the life chances of organizations. Another chapter deals with processes of decline and turnaround. Three chapters in the present volume review the major life-threatening pathologies, which are organizational politics, organizational corruption, and organizational crime. The book also contains chapters on crises and fixations, on failure and survival, and on processes of disbandment and closure of dying organizations. The consideration of these issues follows a diagnostic model of failure, proposed in the introduction to the book.

Organizational Pathology: Life and Death of Organizations should serve a variety of readers. The book is primarily intended to assist students and scholars, in the social and behavioral sciences, who are interested in the study of organizations. It is also intended to similarly serve students and scholars in business and/or public administration, as well as those in the field of management. Practitioners may find in this book some facts about the causes and consequences of organizational downfall, with which they may not have been previously familiar. Organizational consultants can use the book for clues that foreshadow decline, directions on how to diagnose certain symptoms of abnormal behavior, and signs of decline or failure among their clients.

Although this volume is addressed to readers who are familiar with the study and/or with the practice of organizations, I have tried to write it in a friendly style so that it will be of value to a wide range of readers with different professional backgrounds. To illustrate the rather abstract concepts and arguments, I used various real-life examples of events that occurred in several countries and were quoted in the mass media. To avoid unnecessary offenses, I do not mention the names of specific countries, organizations, or individuals in this volume unless they were widely published elsewhere.

Just as my previous book on organizational politics led to the subject's inclusion in the university curriculum, it is my hope that this book will encourage the initiation of academic courses on the study of organizational pathology.

1

A Theoretical Framework

Social scientists are well aware of the fact that a considerable proportion of organizations disappear eventually. Many of them come to an end while they are still young. An enormous number of businesses fail and go bankrupt every year in the USA, Europe, Asia, and elsewhere. In one way or another, many large-scale airlines, high-technology enterprises, publishing houses, and retail chains have become extinct during the last several years. The global financial crisis of the present time demonstrates how giant financial institutions, industrial corporations and global businesses can collapse one after the other like a house of cards.

Likewise, all over the world, numerous non-profit organizations often dissolve (e.g., trade unions, political parties). Plenty of them simply fade out, barely leaving a trace behind. Even governmental agencies and state owned corporations are not immune. Many are privatized and transformed into business companies (e.g., defense industries). A huge number of organizations are compelled to downsize repeatedly. All of these events indicate that the life expectancy of organizations tends to be rather short.

The topic of organizations' success appears to draw more scholarly interest than does the subject of their failure. There seem to be many publications that address the issue of organizational growth than that of organizational decline. This suggests that the notion of organizational birth is more popular in the literature on organizations than that of organizational death.

It is not surprising that positive consequences are usually more appealing for discussion than negative ones. Practitioners prefer to look for strategies and tactics that can make organizations more effective, adaptive, and competitive. Failures tend to be disregarded, as if they were fatal misfortunes that could not be prevented, and therefore are abandoned without further examination.

Nonetheless, gradually the issues of decline, failure, and death are being incorporated into the literature on organization and management (e.g., Argenti, 1976; Whetten, 1988; Guy, 1989; Weitzel and Jonsson, 1989; Meyer and Zucker, 1989; Anheier, 1999; Mellahi and Wilkinson, 2004).

This volume focuses on several pathological aspects of organizations, such as malfunctions, deficiencies, and disorders, which lead to the quietus of organizations as live entities. In an attempt to discuss the conditions under which organizations go out of business, this study examines states and processes that are likened to mortal diseases in biology and to disorders in psychology. In other words, the book is devoted to the exploration of organizational pathologies and the likelihood of death.

Deficiencies and malfunctions, which endanger the strength and survival of organizations, are treated here as pathologies. Organizational crime, corruption, and other related phenomena are similarly dealt with in this context, as representing abnormalities that threaten the existence of organizations. Some scholars argue that for organizations, politics are a normal part of life (e.g., Clegg, 1996); on the other hand, others consider politics to be detrimental to the wellbeing of organizations (e.g., Mintzberg, 1983). In this volume, the perils of politics are discussed. Once these and similar concepts are viewed as pathological conditions and manifestations, it becomes necessary to analyze them within a proper framework.

One may wonder why it is necessary to pay any attention to such fatal problems, which represent the dark side of organizations, or to deal with unpleasant issues such as these. According to the law of entropy, all systems are doomed to fall apart eventually; organizations are no exception. Therefore, scientists and practitioners alike should endeavor to make the most of organizations while they are alive and avoid the dead ones. However, there is another outlook that views organizational pathologies as natural events, which should by no means be ignored.

Evidently, no one casts doubt on the indispensable contribution of pathology to medical research and practice. Similarly, the knowledge acquired through the study of pathology in psychology is essential for understanding and treating mental disorders. In the present view, then, organizational pathology should have a similar role in the study of organizations.

Acquiring a better understanding of the causes and consequences of organizational deficiencies, malfunctions, decline processes, and internal abnormalities may help us predict such problems in advance, assess their severity, apply proper remedies to the extent they are available, avoid the escalation of crisis situations, and postpone the final demise of failing organizations by means of turnaround plans.

The ecological study of organizations sets out to explain birth and death rates in large-scale populations from a historical perspective. In contrast, the study of organizational pathologies focuses on a single organization or on small samples in an attempt to unfold the sequence of fatal problems, not unlike the study of disease etiology in medicine. The ecological approach looks for contextual and external predictive variables, such as the organizations' age, size, industry, and ownership; the pathological approach, which seeks explanatory variables, considers factors such as leadership and management, strategy, structure, and culture. These two perspectives and their empirical findings are discussed in this volume as complementary elements.

Organizations are perceived here as if they were natural systems, while it is acknowledged that they are not really so. "Organizations [as natural systems] are collectivities whose participants share a common interest in the survival of the system and who engage in collective activities, informally structured, to secure this end" (Scott, 1992:25).

From this vantage point, organizations are regarded as live organisms, whose structure and behavior are mostly determined by their need to survive. Organizations accordingly undergo various changes to cope with the constraints of their environments, as do living organisms in nature. While we follow this line of thought, we should bear in mind that organizations are by no means biological systems of any kind; therefore, this analogy should not be carried too far.

The image of organizations as natural systems has led some scholars to develop the so-called *life-cycle paradigm* (e.g., Chandler, 1962; Greiner, 1972; Adizes, 1979; Block and Galbraith, 1982; Churchill and Lewis, 1983; Quinn and Cameron, 1983; Miller and Friesen, 1984; Block and MacMillan, 1985; Kazanjian, 1988; Kazanjian and Drazin, 1989; Hanks, 1990). "Traditionally, scholars have used a biological analog to explain the growth patterns of organizations" (Kazanjian, 1998:257). Accordingly, the literature on the organizational life cycle claims that organizations develop through certain stages of maturation, which manifest in a stepwise process: from the first stage, birth, to the last stage, death. In each life-cycle stage, the organization displays a unique set of typical features (Adizes, 1988). A life-cycle stage is defined as "a unique configuration of variables related to the organization's context and structure" (Hanks, Watson, Jansen, and Chandler, 1994:7). Proponents of this paradigm generally agree that organizations evolve in stages, but they disagree about the number and the nature of these life stages.

The life-cycle model rests on the assumption that living organisms, organizations, as well other open systems are all subject to a life-cycle destiny. They are born, grow, mature, age, and eventually die. The sequential changes that occur in organizations represent evolutionary stages; in other words, the process is similar to the biological life cycle found in nature (Daft, 2004).

The life-cycle paradigm is well established in the literature. Although not accepted by all, it is widely discussed (see, for example, Whetten, 1987). The findings presented in the relevant literature indicate that organizations evolve in a consistent and predictable manner. They move from one stage to the next, by making appropriate changes in their structure and function. These structural transformations enable them to cope with problems entailed in the process of growth. Typically, this process in organizations involves a great deal of pain, sometimes even severe crises (Greiner, 1972).

Students of organizations portray different models of the organizational life cycle, describing stages of growth and development. They emphasize the unique set of characteristics that typifies each stage. More important than the different number of stages that each model presents is the fact that these stages (1) are sequential, (2) follow a hierarchical progression, and (3) involve a range of organizational activities and structures (Quinn and Cameron, 1983). Table 1.1 compares various models of organizational life-cycle proposed in the literature.

Once organizations are treated as natural systems, they are presumably bound to meet their end at one time or another; this is obviously the last stage of their life cycle. Organizations as systems are subject to the second law of thermodynamics—"the law of entropy" (Katz and Kahn, 1978; Scott, 1992). Yet, regardless of whether all organizations must die, it is quite likely that most of those that do reach their demise do so "unnaturally," due to incurable conditions. Borrowing from the medical language, such a condition is called an *organizational pathology*. Pathology is usually defined as "an abnormal condition or biological state in which proper functioning is prevented" (Reber, 1985:521). The concept also serves as a general label for the scientific study of such conditions. Keeping to this language, the following chapters address the *pathogenesis* of organizational death, namely, they discuss the mechanisms by which certain factors give rise to various terminal diseases.

Table 1.1
Comparison of Life-Cycle Stage Models: Names and Numbers of Stages

Model	Start Up Stage	Expansion Stage	Maturity Stage	Diversification Stage	Decline Stage
Adizes, 1989	1. Courtship 2. Infancy	3. Go-Go 4. Adolescence	5. Prime 6. Stable		7. Aristocracy 8. Early Bureaucracy 9. Bureaucracy 10. Death
Churchill & Lewis, 1983	1. Existence 2. Survival 3(D). Success-Disengagement	3(G). Success-Growth 4. Take-Off	5. Resource Maturity		
Flamholtz, 1987	1. New Venture	2. Expansion	3. Professionalization 4. Consolidation	5. Diversification 6. Integration	7. Decline
Galbraith,1982	1. Proof of Principle/Prototype 2. Model Shop	3. Start-Up/Volume Production	4. Natural Growth	5. Strategic Maneuvering	
Greiner, 1972	1. Creativity	2. Direction	3. Delegation	4. Coordination 5. Collaboration	
Kazanjian, 1988	1. Conception & Development 2. Commercialization	3. Growth	4. Stability		
Miller & Friesen, 1984b	1. Birth	2. Growth	3. Maturity	4. Revival	5. Decline
Quinn & Cameron, 1983	1. Entrepreneurial	2. Collectivity	3. Formalization	4. Elaboration of Structure	
Scott & Bruce, 1987	1. Inception 2. Survival	3. Growth 4. Expansion	5. Maturity		
Smith, Mitchell, & Summer, 1985	1. Inception	2. High Growth	3. Maturity		

Source: Hanks, S. H., Watson, C. J., Jansen, E. and G. N. Chandler."Tightening the Life-Cycle Construct: A Taxonomic Study of Growth Stage Configurations in High-Technology Organizations." *Entrepreneurship Theory and Practice*, 1993 (Winter), Vol. 17 (5). Reproduced with the permission of Blackwell Publishing.

Similar to individuals, organizations may suffer prolonged, severe pathologies that do not necessarily lead to death. One such type of pathology is known in medicine as *chronic disease*. In organizations, the equivalent of chronic disease takes the form of an enduring deficiency in the production or the support subsystems. Despite these problems, long-lasting organizations find ways to adapt to these deficiencies and to go on with their tasks. They bypass chronic conditions by concealing them from the public gaze and by adjusting the budget and workforce allocated to the deficient subsystems. For example, "when management's goal is to maximize achievement of the organization's mission, it is practical to remove resources from the unit failing to contribute to the effort and reallocate to those units which do" (Guy, 1989:16).

Where there are inherent defects, an organization cannot completely heal. The challenge before management in such cases is to contain the problem within bearable limits. The problematic component is separated as much as possible from the mainstream, to minimize its counterproductive effects. That is the well-known strategy of *loose coupling* (Orton and Weick, 1990). In some cases, the "sick organ" is wholly excised from the organization's "body," by its termination or by selling it off.

Another analogy that can be used in this context of non-terminal pathologies is based on the phenomena of *personality disorders* in the realm of psychology. Individuals who suffer from such disorders usually are capable of maintaining their routine life, communicating with family members and friends, and performing various tasks. The seemingly normal life may continue for many years, although it carries a great deal of hidden pain, functional difficulties, and recurring anxieties. Organizations' participants may display behavior patterns that are analogous to symptoms of personality disorder. Some examples of such pathologies are doing things only "by the book;" following superiors' instructions at the expense of clients' needs and against the public interest; and stubborn resistance to change—even when it is, admittedly, much needed (Scott, 1992).

This point in the introduction is an appropriate place to present the author's theoretical framework that guides this volume. It is portrayed graphically in Figure 1.1.

As a point of departure, it is assumed here that two sets of factors make a considerable impact on organizations' chances of survival. These factors are internal and external. The former reside within the organization itself, and are designated in the literature as *r-extinction*; the latter reside in the organization's environment, and are designated in the literature as *k-extinction*.

Figure 1.1
A Diagnostic Framework of Organizational Failure

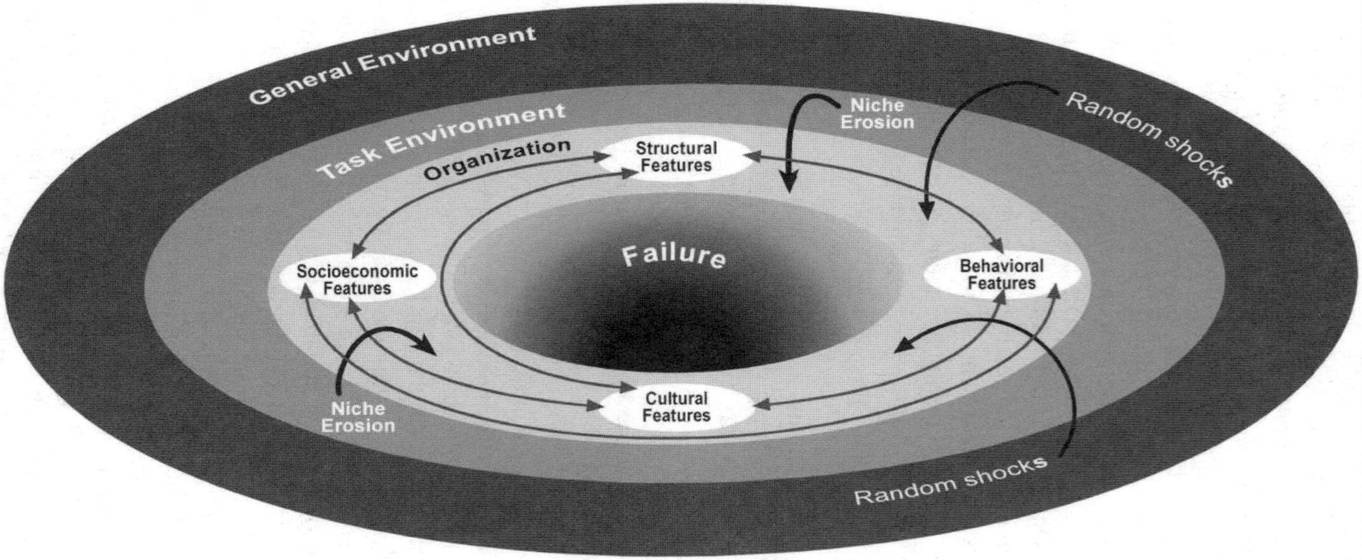

Organizations should be conceptualized as open systems. As such, they are embedded in economic, political, social, and technological environments simultaneously. While organizational environments have been classified in many ways, in the present context they are broadly classified according to only two main groups: the *task environment* and the *general environment*. The *task environment* is that with which the organization interacts directly. "The task environment typically includes the industry, raw materials, and market sectors, and perhaps the human resources and the international sectors." The general environment includes "those sectors that might not have direct impact on the daily operations of a firm but will indirectly influence it. The general environment often includes the government, socio-cultural, economic conditions, technology and financial resources sectors" (Daft, 2004:137-8).

The task environment of organizations consists of various market niches (e.g., fast food, daily newspapers, fancy cars, etc.) in which a certain population of organizations makes its living. An *organizational niche*, then, contains a certain combination of various resources (e.g., raw materials, human resources) that carry those organizations and enable them to survive. Depletion of the niche resources jeopardizes the survival chances of those organizations. In fact, such niche erosion affects both birth and death rates of organizations. Organizations are likely to fail whenever their particular niche can no longer carry them, for whatever reason.

The general environment is usually more remote than the task environment, but influential nevertheless. The general environment affects organizations' chances of survival by virtue of the "random shocks" it may deliver: large-scale external crises of various kinds, such as a sudden war, a coup, some natural disaster, or an economic crash. Although such random shocks impinge upon organizations indirectly, they serve as *trigger effects*, which bring some organizations to a state of bankruptcy, breakdown, or quick collapse. Even the survivors are vulnerable to loss of clientele, shortage of supplies, and shrinkage of their profits. Hence, many suffer from serious problems.

As Figure 1.1 suggests, the wellbeing and survival of organizations presumably depend on the following internal factors: structure, culture, social-economic conditions, and behavioral patterns. Each one of these consists of a set of organizational features representing one dimension of the organization. Taken together, these dimensions enable us to define and diagnose the state of affairs that characterizes a given organization at a given time. Note that the posited relationships between these dimensions represent systemic causal loops, which reinforce one another reciprocally.

Briefly, the structural dimension of organizations represents features such as functional differentiation, centralization, formalization, and hierarchization of the organization.

The socioeconomic dimension of organizations consists of parameters reflecting their social strength in terms of quantity and quality of the human resource (e.g., size of the work force and its level of education). It also indicates the economic vigor of organizations (e.g., assets, investments, and slack resources). In addition, this complex dimension indicates organizations' market position (e.g., market share, sales volume, and backlog of orders).

The cultural dimension of organizations represents basic assumptions (e.g., the organization's mission), main values (e.g., service, innovation), and social norms (e.g., loyalty, reciprocity). These and similar features are believed to govern the participants' conduct.

Strategic choices; leadership and managerial styles, employment policy, use or abuse of environmental resources; often reveal the behavioral dimension of organizations. In the present context, organizational behavior refers primarily to the ways in which executives and managers actually lead their organizations to the attainment of their goals. As elaborated in the following chapters, bad management causes a large proportion of organizational failures, in both the private and the public sector.

With this diagnostic framework in mind, the next chapters analyze the pathogenesis that accounts for various organizational problems and their outcomes. This volume attempts to diagnose some organizational processes (e.g., politics, corruption, crime) that jeopardize organizations' chances of survival, propel their failure, and cause their eventual demise. As part of the present endeavor, and based on the relevant literature, issues such as the various forms of organizational death, their predictors, and their antecedents receive special attention in this volume.

From the present viewpoint, then, the notion of organizational pathology serves as an encompassing concept that attempts to account for the conditions liable to lead to organizational failure and cessation.

2

Organizational Fatality

Collapsed, failed, bankrupt, broke, and bust. None of these are pleasant words, and this is not a pleasant subject, but in real life companies do collapse, they do fail, and do "go bust." And yet, how often does one see these words in books or articles on management? Hardly ever—it is most extraordinary. It is not only books: one cannot attend a lecture on the causes of failure as one can on every other conceivable management topic; one cannot consult an expert on the subject for there are virtually none. (Argenti, 1976:1)

Since this observation was published over thirty years ago, some change has taken place in the study of management and of organization. Nowadays, one can find quite a few analytical essays on this subject, some theoretical models of organizational decline, as well as quite a few empirical studies of organizational mortality. Some of these publications will be referred to in this volume. Several instances of organizational collapse of large corporations (e.g., Rolls-Royce in the United Kingdom; Enron in the United States) were so astonishing that their stories have been documented as case studies. Nevertheless, MBA classes devoted to organizations' failure, collapse, or disintegration are few even today. Nor do any pathologies rate much attention.

It has already been explained that the main reason for ignoring this issue lies in the deep-rooted value of success in contemporary Western culture (e.g., Argenti, 1976; Whetten, 1980). Broadly stated, the "sickness" and "death" of organizations tends to be attributed to incompetent leadership and poor management. It is not surprising that nobody likes to be associated with failure. A popular proverb says, "Success has many fathers, but failure is always an orphan."

In the United States during the years 2000 to 2005 approximately 544,000 business firms deceased every year. Of these, approximately 37,000 per year were officially recorded as bankruptcies. During the same time period, approximately 630,000 new business firms were born annually (U.S. Bureau of Census 2007, Table 744).

A recent intriguing book presents an interesting set of data on the world's largest one hundred industrial companies. The figures reveal that over the period of 1912 to 1995, forty-eight of these companies disappeared; out of these, twenty-nine companies went bankrupt; fifty-two companies survived; and only nineteen companies remained in the top one hundred in 1995. "The period 1912 to 1995 is not much longer than the average life expectancy of a human being" (Ormerod, 2006:14). In other words, the chances of a large, rich, and well-established business organization being able to survive is about the same as its chances of demise.

This chapter discusses the termination of organizations as distinctive and active entities; that is, when they neither provide products nor render services—they cease to function. The fundamental question in the study of pathology, whether in biological organisms or in organizational entities, is the meaning of death. In practice, the key question is on what grounds a once-living system may be acceptably determined as dead. In medicine, to assess if a body is still alive health professionals measure various vital signs. Apparently, such vital signs have not yet been established with regard to organizations. The notion of *organizational death* is therefore rather complicated, since in reality the end of an organization may come in quite different forms, some of them still are controversial among scholars as they were twenty-five years ago.

> While research on organizational death is beginning to emerge in the literature (Kaufman 1976; Hall 1976; Aldrich and Reiss 1976; Behn 1976), it is hampered by a lack of consensus on what organizational death represents. Does it occur when there is a change in the name of an organization? When all its members are replaced? When the facility is moved? Does it make a difference if these events are the result of a merger, as compared with a business failure? (Whetten in Kimberley, et al., 1980:371)

In the business sector organizations come to an end mainly due to a state of insolvency or of *bankruptcy*. The legal act bankruptcy requires the owners of a business firm to surrender their property to the benefit of its creditors, by authorizing an outside trustee to manage its financial activities to pay debts. For instance, between the years 2000 to 2006, the total number of bankruptcy cases filed in the U.S. courts increased from 1,276,900 in 2000 to 1,637,300 in 2005 (U.S. Bureau of Census 2007, Table 755). Bankrupt organizations are likely to disappear from the business scene once their assets, tangible and intangible, are given away to the creditors.

Quite often business organizations disappear through a process of dismantling. This form of organizational death is usually manifested when a failing organization is purchased cheap solely for the purpose of its liquidation. The entire organization is broken down into separate components (e.g., product lines, installations, strategic business units, or divisions) that are sold off piecemeal to different clients. Needless to say, once this dismantling is done the initial organization will never be restored as before. Therefore, we will refer to such a termination as death by *organizational disintegration*. Whether this act of elimination occurs due to bankruptcy or acquisition, the splitting of the organization into its parts inevitably brings about its demise (cf., Anheier 1999).

While organizational disintegration as just described here is typical in the realm of business, it also occurs, although not as frequently, in the realm of politics. Political parties in many democratic countries disintegrate due to splitting into several components; then each joins its forces with other political parties. Even nation states are broken into several ethnically defined pieces, which establish themselves as separate sovereign states. The case of the former Yugoslavia, which was broken after furious military fighting and heavy casualties, presents a typical example of the disintegration of a nation state.

Organizational takeover is another well-known strategy of hiding a business firm under the cover of a different organization, most likely a rival, by means of acquisition or merger. Although the captive organization may remain intact, in terms of its components and/or its productive activities, it no longer exists as an independent entity. From some points of view, the outcome of such an act is considered certain death. First, the business firm has lost the commercial name by which it was recognized in the market. Second, it is no longer allowed to use its trademark(s) publicly, since it is required to adopt the new owner's trademark instead. Third, in some cases even the brand name of the firm's products must be changed for advertising purposes. Fourth, the name of the previous owner is most likely removed from the firm and its products. Under these and similar conditions the firm becomes deeply submerged, so for all practical purposes it no longer exists as a distinct business entity. This form of death is most likely to occur when a giant corporation takes over a small business firm.

Like human beings, organizations may experience a fatal event—a type of "stroke"—that causes their rapid collapse. *Organizational collapse* may be seen as another form of death in the realm of organizations. Naturally, this kind of events is not preplanned, often not even foreseen, by the management or the owner of such an organization. In many cases such strokes occur in consequence of extreme environmental conditions such as a devastating war (e.g., the war in Iraq), a mega-terror attack (e.g., September 11th), natural disasters (e.g., tsunami, earthquake), stock market collapse (e.g., the "hi-tech bubble"), and the like. On the other hand, organizations suffer such unexpected strokes due to some internal failure (e.g., breakdown of a major technological component), mismanagement (erroneous investment in a certain currency or commodity), or corruption (public disclosure of an enormous fraud). Organizational collapse is then most likely to occur, leading, in turn, to the disappearance of the organization as a live and active entity. The following examples of such catastrophic outcomes may illumine the death of organizations through organizational collapse.

Here is one example: in a small bank an employee discovered a secret way to withdraw varying amounts of money from clients' accounts without their knowledge. For a period of five years that employee gradually withdrew about a quarter billion in local currency (the equivalence of fifty million U.S. Dollars then) to cover the astronomic debts of her brother, an addicted gambler, to several casinos around the world. For whatever reason, she voluntarily went to the police and disclosed her huge theft. Once this information was reported in the media, it took no longer than a few days for the bank to collapse. As dictated by the law of that country, the bank was forced to shut down and its financial activities have never been resumed.

Numerous not-for-profit organizations (e.g., trade unions, political parties, and voluntary associations) are susceptible to the damages of random shocks. For most of them, two kinds of resources are critical: members and budgets. A main existential problem of such organizations is the gradual shrinkage of the body of active membership. People tend to tire of continually having to invest their time and energy in such organizations; many of them become disappointed with these organizations and their partly attainments; other people change their interests and priorities with the passage of time. There is always an outflow of members from such organizations, a natural trend that proves fatal when the stream of exiting members suddenly swells to a critical volume, which is most likely to happen at times of some internal or external crisis. For organizations whose revenue comes primarily from membership fees, or from members' donations, the situation gets even worse. Under such circumstances of *membership drain,* the organization's death is imminent.

For example, a national federation of labor unions, with which the vast majority of employees had been affiliated for many years, used to provide healthcare services to its members. In 1994, a new law of National Health

Care came into effect. According to this law, every citizen of the country has the right to get healthcare services regardless of his or her affiliation, if at all, with any labor union. Consequently, that federation of the labor unions lost about a quarter million of its members in a rather short period of time, merely because they were no longer dependent on labor unions for healthcare services. As the federation encountered serious financial problems, leading to a severe crisis, it was compelled to divest most of its assets, losing its enormous power. To turn around that giant "sinking ship" and avoid total collapse, a painful organizational reorientation and transformation were performed. The so-called New Federation of Workers is certainly a different entity than it was in the past.

Last but not least, the tendency of organizations to conduct far-reaching changes turns them into essentially different entities from those they used to be in more ways than one. In their attempt to conduct reorientation, reengineering, restructuring, and the like, organizations replace their old definitions of mission, culture, structure, and even their main business. However, we should be aware that the end result of a profound change of this magnitude may be the creation of a new organization in place of the old one. In that case, the previous organization no longer exists. Whatever the new character of the changed organization may be, it is fundamentally different from the one it was prior to the change. From this aspect, *organizational transformation* may be seen as a form of organizational death. This conclusion may not be accepted by some scholars or practitioners who are adherents of organizational change. Nevertheless, in the biological sciences the whole idea of transformation, or metamorphosis, is a complete change in the structure and nature of an organization. The probable price of such a renewal is the removal of the obsolete form.

In light of such events, it seems plausible to argue that the pronouncement of an organization's death can be made only after some time. Since organizations are not, in fact, biological organisms, those that appear moribund may revive after a while, probably due to some program of turnaround. It takes time to conclude whether or not an organization has perished.

Consider the following example: On November 2003 a well-known baby food firm, named "Remedia," sold vegetarian substitute of mother's milk, made from soybeans, in which the quantity of vitamin B1 had been reduced in the contents of the formula. Remedia did not notify the babies' parents of this change. Shortly afterwards three infants died and twenty babies had to be hospitalized for diagnosis and treatment due to then unknown symptoms. The Ministry of Health conducted a quick inspection and the cause of these sicknesses was identified, namely, shortage of the essential vitamin in the new formula. Thousands of consumers stopped purchasing the product at once. The cans were immediately removed from stores. Lawsuits against the producer were prepared; parents held open protests; accusations were voiced on all sides, and a loud public debate on the ethical integrity of producers of such sensitive products could be heard on every radio and television channel. Consequently, consumers boycotted a variety of products sold by that firm. In a very short time, this firm (a domestic branch of a global corporation) went out of business. For all that, the firm was subsequently acquired from the global corporation by a domestic investor, and it was started anew. The new owner has kept the old brand name, but the acquisition contract frees him of any responsibility for the consequences of the last owners' scandalous behavior. The new business resumed production and marketing of the same products formerly supplied by the deceased organization. The old managerial staff, dismissed at the time of the crisis, has been replaced. Clearly, the new organization is by no means the old one. Nevertheless, the current firm has not been doing well, apparently because of the stigma attached to products carrying the same brand name. Although death is usually regarded as a one-off event, expiring is a somewhat progressive process that under some circumstances may be prolonged. Like biological organisms, dying organizations displaying some signs indicating that death is most likely to occur soon. The dying process has been addressed in the literature on organizations mainly under the term *organizational decline* (e.g., Cameron, Whetten, and Kim, 1987; Whetten, 1988; Cameron, Sutton, and Whetten, 1988). Briefly, an organization undergoing this pathological process is likely to progress in stages toward its end (Weitzel and Jonsson, 1989). In light of its importance for the understanding of organizational pathology, an entire chapter of this volume is devoted to the issue of decline.

The process of dying or the decline of organizations does not necessarily lead to instantaneous collapse. Some do recover at a certain stage, provided an appropriate organizational response is applied in time (Weitzel and Jonsson, 1991). Mary Guy (1989) nicely labeled this kind of turnaround—resurrection as she calls it—*the Phoenix Syndrome*, concluding, "it is the rare firm that does not go through a cyclical pattern of declines and resurrections" (Guy, 1989:12). She presents the history of Federal Express as a typical example of this life-cycle pattern, consisting of such ups and downs.

Nevertheless, many organizations that are caught in the downward spiral of decline are doomed to pass away, at least when they reach "the point of no return" in that process. This is the stage of severe crisis, from which renewal becomes so difficult that the organization no longer has the necessary energy to fight for its survival. Organizations at that stage are likely to display symptoms of exhaustion, shortage of critical resources, inadaptability, and loss of self-control. Under such conditions, organizations, like organisms, should be classified as displaying a distinct form of death, even if this effect takes a considerable time to be completed.

These forms of organizational death demonstrate the complexity of this concept—on the theoretical as well as the practical level. Viewed from the population-ecology perspective, the notion of organizational death was defined as follows:

> An organization dissolves when it ceases to carry out the routine actions that sustain its structure, maintain flows of resources, and retain the allegiance of its members. A labor union that still has a charter and a national office but no labor contracts, no members, and no organizers is a dead union. Similarly, a firm that retains a corporate identity and an address but does not have a staff other than a skeleton office staff is no longer a firm. (Freeman, Carroll and Hannan, 1983:694)

In most cases the termination of organizations as viable entities, of one kind or another, is the outcome of *organizational failure*. However, failure does not necessarily mean final termination. In fact, more than a few "permanently failing organizations" are to be found everywhere; they do not fade from the organizational scene (Meyer and Zucker, 1989). Prisons represent one example of permanently failing organizations. This concept denotes poor performance of an organization, which proves unable to attain its predetermined concrete goals and objectives. Such results are gauged by financial measures (e.g., profits), business measures (market share), or economic measures (assets).

> For the organizational approach, the concept of failure is not inherently ambiguous and problematic...Nonetheless, it should in most cases be possible to use economic performance and activity criteria to measure organizational failure. This does not mean, however, that we treat organizational failure as a finite phenomenon. It can be the absolute end, or dissolution, of a firm. However, it can also lead to persistently low performance or profound reorganization. Most authors in the field distinguish between two types of failure: transformation and closure. Firms "transform" when they merge, lose independent control, and change of ownership. "Closure" results from the loss of a corporate charter, bankruptcy, and mission completion. (Anheier and Moulton, 1999:274-276)

Similarly, the Dun and Bradstreet Corporation, which collects ongoing weekly statistics of business failures, explains how it includes failed organizations in its datasets: "Business failures do not represent total business closings, which consist of both business failures and business discontinuances. As defined by Dun & Bradstreet's statistics, business failures consist of businesses involved in court proceedings or voluntary actions involving losses to creditors" (Dun & Bradstreet Failure Record, 1997:19).

In the public sector, failure (or success) may be indicated by the number of voters for a political party, by the number of members of a labor union, or by the number of scientific publications of a university. Sport clubs, voluntary associations, philanthropic funds, public libraries, and other not-for-profit organizations adopt their own criteria of success and failure, which are meaningful in the context of their particular environmental niches.

According to Anheier and Moulton (Anheier, 1999), the themes of failure, breakdown, and bankruptcy have been studied by scholars mainly from four different perspectives: organizational, political, cognitive, and structural.

From the *organizational* viewpoint, death is the inevitable last stage of the organizational life cycle. The life-cycle approach attributes success and failure to the fit, or lack of it, between management and performance and environmental conditions.

From the *political* perspective, organizations are political entities struggling for power and influence. An organization's failure and demise are mainly caused by an inability to gain and maintain legitimacy.

Regarding *cognitive* aspects, studies focusing on these "deal with questions of perception, identification, and declaration of failure" (Anheier, 1999:6). Students of this approach seek psychological dispositions and expectations of executives, which may affect the likelihood of failure.

The *structural* perspective focuses on organizations' social fabric. From this viewpoint, relational elements such as conflict and antagonism among the members of and groups in organizations create tendencies to failure. Such built-in tendencies do not necessarily coincide with economic problems. The notion of structural failure denotes a social state of affairs or a certain pattern of social relations within an organization.

Numerous organizations die everyday, so one may rightly wonder whether organizations at death's door resemble organic systems afflicted by terminal illnesses. In the next chapters this query is discussed in greater detail. At this point it seems plausible to assume that they do; processes of organizational decline, especially in their last stages, display similar symptoms to biological bodies dying in nature. Organizations also tend to collapse abruptly, just as organisms die from a sudden stroke, rapid suffocation, or a fatal accident. These causes of demise receive due attention in the present volume as well.

Conclusion

The idea of organizational fatality stems from the fact that organizations, like other social, economic, and political systems, are eventually doomed to die. Organizations of whatever kind are subject to the law of entropy, like all other systems. However, being open systems that exchange needed resources with their environment, they have the capacity to delay their death for a very long time (i.e., *negentropy*). The best example of surviving for impressively long time is the Catholic Church. Still, internal and external disturbances subject organizations to severe pressures, which cause their dissolution in one way or another. Evidently, ancient empires that ruled major parts of the world for hundreds years came to their end and disappeared forever.

As described in this chapter, probably the most common way of dying in the realm of organizations nowadays is through bankruptcy, sometimes called insolvency. This legal term refers to the declared inability of an organization to pay its debts to creditors, such as suppliers, contractors, employees, and the like.

Organizations may end their lives as viable, whole entities due to their disintegration. This form of organizational death is usually manifest when a failing organization is acquired solely for the purpose of its liquidation. Such an organization, or its remaining parts, is sold out piece by piece to different clients, each of them interested in purchasing a certain component.

Another form of death is by takeover, acquisition, or merger, in which an entire organization is swallowed by another, frequently a large-scale corporation. The absorbing organization is likely to reframe the new firm as a division, wiping out most of the previous recognizable signs.

Organizations sometimes fall apart all at once due to an unexpected or unforeseen event, such as the sudden outbreak of war or a natural disaster. This form of organizational death resembles fatal strokes that suddenly attack biological organisms, bringing about their death in a very short time.

Massive exit of organizational members or supporters drags organizations down to their end by a continuous process of shrinkage. This form of death is more likely to occur in the public sector, where labor unions, voluntary associations, political parties, and so forth are active.

The death of an organization, in whatever way, is closely associated with organizational failure: its inability to attain its goals, accomplish its objectives, or obtain sufficient resources critical for its survival. Failure, then, may be considered to represent a fatal event or a pathological process in an organization's life cycle. The question accordingly arises as to how and why organizations fail so badly as to endanger their lives.

3

Failure Prediction Models

In this chapter the role of four major variables of organizations—age, size, niche, and performance—are discussed. The underlying assumption is that these variables serve as predictors, rather than determinants, of death rates among organizations. Because they are not pathogenic deficiencies or malfunctions per se, so they should not be regarded as necessary and sufficient conditions for the death of organizations. Instead, they represent certain conditions under which organizations might be in greater or lesser danger of losing their lives. In this sense, they are *contextual variables*, in the sense that they facilitate or impede the development of strengths or weaknesses, such as the ability to change or the tendency to innovate.

Looking at these variables, as several scholars who studied this area have done, enables one to understand better the situations in which organizations are prone to collapse. For example, let us consider the age factor. Following the life-cycle paradigm, at least two life stages immediately come to mind, namely, infancy and old age. Similarly, the size factor points to very small and very large organizations as fertile soil for high mortality rates. We shall now elaborate these contextual variables, and assess their role as catalysts of organizational death.

The Age Factor

The successful birth of organizations is by no means a guarantee of their survival. In fact, over half of newborn business enterprises die in the early years of their life. A considerable proportion of them do not survive even one year. The data on organizational mortality in the United States, the United Kingdom, and the European Union reveal that new business organizations are much more likely to collapse than old ones. In the United States, for instance, about 54 percent survive for just eighteen months, about 25 percent last five to six years, and approximately 20 percent remain in business over ten years. Thus, one-quarter of all business enterprises are less than one year old, and the average age is only seven years (Aldrich and Auster, 1986:177; Van de Ven, 1980:83). Apparently, newly started organizations suffer from various weaknesses due to their lack of the necessary means to cope with their environmental threats.

Over forty years ago, the sociologist Arthur Stinchcombe (1965) coined the term *liability of newness* to describe the syndrome that characterizes young organizations and to account for their high rates of mortality. The liability of organizations is the result of several deficiencies, which are typical of those at the entrepreneurial stage of their lives. The first deficiency is the lack of well-established roles and positions in which their occupants' tasks and responsibilities are defined. Moreover, most of the new organization's participants have to learn how to do their jobs without proper training and no predecessors who can share their experience with them. The learning process involves many human errors, personal tensions, and interpersonal disagreements about the proper way to perform these jobs. The second deficiency is improper implementation of various formal procedures (e.g., manufacturing, maintenance, reporting of financial activities, and control procedures), which require long preparation. Meanwhile, at least some of the operations are managed efficiently enough to ensure smooth supply of raw materials, equipment, and revenues. The third shortcoming is the plain need of young organizations to rely on interpersonal cooperation and coordination among individuals who are not familiar with one another, whose mutual trust has not yet been established, who are unable to assess correctly the values or the motives of their fellow workers. Last but not least, new organizations lack longstanding relationships with external stakeholders (e.g., clients, suppliers, agents). They must cope with their task environment without the support of networks (Stinchcombe, 1965:148-150).

In light of this liability of newness it is no wonder that business organizations in their initial phase of life are exposed to severe hardship, threatening their survival. Predictably, a high rate of them will soon collapse, as statistical evidence on organizational mortality confirms. Yet, as much as this argument makes sense theoretically, research attempts to support it empirically do not provide consistent results as one would expect. Apparently, the correlation between age and mortality is neither linear nor monotonic. Let us take a closer look at the relationship between organizations' age and mortality.

The liability of newness has received the attention of organizational ecologists, who have conducted quite a few studies of this proposition from their perspective. Earlier studies done in the 1980s provided repeated empirical support for the liability of newness argument (e.g., Carroll and Delacroix, 1982; Freeman, Carroll, and Hannan, 1983; Carroll, 1984; Carroll, 1987). They suggested that organizations face a declining likelihood of death with the passing of time. This trend has been modeled as a continuous-decline monotonic function. Carroll concluded, "Markham's Law, a stochastic model of the hazard function with age-dependent properties, is becoming accepted as the baseline model for the study of organizational mortality" (Carroll, 1984:85). However, there seem to be some doubts with regard to the age-dependence argument.

The question of age dependence in the rate of organizational mortality is the feature of organizational ecology that has been most extensively examined empirically. The basic empirical regularity that emerges is that the risk of mortality tends to decline with organizational age. However, despite prominence in ecological analysis, there has been little explicit modeling of time-varying organizational-level processes which, in turn, lead to predictions of population-level rates of mortality. (Levinthal, 1991:397)

Moreover, some later empirical studies did not find the expected monotonic decline of organizational mortality as a function of age (e.g., Singh, House, and Tucker, 1986; Carroll and Huo, 1986; Halliday, Powell, and Granfors, 1987; Barnett and Carroll, 1987; King and Wicker, 1988; Aldrich, 1979; Fichman and Levinthal, 1991). They raised questions concerning the generality of the liability-of-newness proposition.

Bruderl and Schussler (1990), in a study of 171,000 business firms in Germany, found that the liability-of-newness hypothesis did not fit business organizations in Germany well. In their thorough analysis of that enormous sample, they found that mortality rates behaved in an inverted U-shape mode in relation to organizational age. More specifically, their findings showed that "depending on the initial resource endowments of a firm, mortality peaks between one and fifteen years after founding" (p. 530). Therefore, they suggested an alternative hypothesis to liability of newness, which co-relates mortality risk to organizations' age. Bruderl and Schussler coined the concept of *liability of adolescence* to describe this non-monotonic function of mortality rates over time.

The rationale for this statistical trend assumes that business organizations begin their life with some stock of initial resources (e.g., seed money), usually endowed to them by investors or contributors of one kind or another. Thus, new business ventures usually have the resources to survive for some length of time, during which they attempt to establish business connections, build a proper structure, and manage as rationally as possible.

> Hence, there are two reasons why the highest risk of disbandment should not be found at the very beginning of an organizational life. The first reason is that organizations can survive because there is an initial stock of resources on which they can live for some time. The second reason is that they will not be abandoned by at least minimally rational actors unless a sufficient amount of negative information about their performance is gathered. The duration of this initial period of waiting for success is not specified by the above-stated argument, but Fichman and Levinthal (1988) and we (Schussler, 1987) claim that it gives rise to a liability of adolescence. (Bruderl and Schussler, 1990:533)

Both "liability of newness" and "liability of adolescence" point to the age-dependence survival of organizations. One explanation for the declining rates of mortality as organizations grow older is ecological. With the passage of time the performance of surviving organizations stabilizes due to learning processes; therefore, they become more reliable and more accountable enterprises from the viewpoint of their clients, their suppliers, and their investors. Consequently, the chances of older organizations surviving "natural selection" processes are higher than those of younger ones.

However, at least one study (Levinthal, 1991) firmly asserts that there is no direct relationship between age and mortality. Levinthal maintains, "the negative relationship between age and mortality rates is due to the fact that older, surviving organizations tend to be organizations that have been successful, and this prior success buffers them from subsequent selection pressures" (p. 399).

The likelihood of death is age-dependent, indeed; the life-cycle paradigm of organizations' development may serve as a model of the successive changes and transformations that they undergo throughout their lifetime. Following this line of thought, one may contemplate the possible "liability of aging" of organizations as well (e.g., Adizes, 1979; 1988).

In keeping with the biological analogy, organizations, like organisms, that reach an advanced age are most likely to die due to the deterioration of their systems. Some scholars term this process of deterioration *organizational decline* (e.g., Cameron, Kim, and Whetten, 1987). However, organizations can experience cycles of decline and incline more than once in their lifetime, not necessarily at old age (Guy, 1989). Still, the concept of the liability of aging may be valid to the extent that declining, elderly organizations face a greater likelihood of death than younger organizations. Guy suggests the following explanation for such a tendency.

Decline in a mature organization may be a result of dysfunctional traditions, customs, or habits that once were functional and contributed to the organizational mission. Such subtle causes of decline take much more time to develop, identify, and rectify. (Guy, 1989:12)

Aged organizations are apparently victims of inertial forces (e.g., risk aversion, maximization of rewards, and bureaucratic culture), which prevent them from making substantial changes to cope with their changing environments (Hannan and Freeman, 1984). Such inertia should, therefore, mainly increase the likelihood of death for aging organizations, which no longer possess the internal flexibility required to adopt new strategies, structures, or cultures. Thus, it seems a plausible assumption that long-standing organizations suffer from the liability of aging, probably in the form of a terminal decline. If so, the mortality rate of aged organizations is likely to rise.

Barron, et al., (1994) draw an analogy to senescence processes observable in animal and human life histories. They suggest that organizations accumulate durable features, such as precedents, political coalitions, and taken-for-granted understandings that constrain modifications in patterns of collective action. Such encrustation erodes the capability for efficient collective action. According to this view, the liability is one of senescence: Mortality rates increase with age. (Hannan, 1998:133)

We recall that the population-ecology approach to the study of organizational mortality analyzes organizational populations. The purpose of such studies is to estimate death rates under various conditions. They by no means depict the life course of specific organizations, while following them over time. Thus, at any age and at every life stage, some organizations pass away whereas others survive under similar conditions.

The Size Factor

Size is probably the most studied variable in the field of organizations, as a variable presumed to affect various features of them. Given the attributed importance of size, it is no wonder that numerous studies have been devoted to the hypothesized relationships between organizations' size and their structure, internal culture, leadership styles, management systems, and participants' behavior patterns.

It, therefore, seems natural to examine the extent to which their size accounts for organizations' survival or demise. For example, students of the population-ecology perspective focus on the co-relation between organizations' size and their rates of death. Before looking at some of the findings, let us bear in mind that the notion of size in organizations consists of more than one dimension. One frequent way of measuring size is to count the number of participants, such as employees or members. Size is also indicated by the number of clients (e.g., the number of a college's students, of a theatre's subscribers, or of a clinic's patients). The physical capacity of an organization serves as a measure of its size, such as the number of a hospital's beds, of a hotel's rooms, or of a supermarket's total length of display shelves.

In the realm of business, indicators like annual sales volume and market share are common representations of a firm's or a corporation's size. Last but not least, organizational size is also estimated by economic and/or financial assets (e.g., total investments). Moreover, "theoretical arguments about organizational size can be divided into two types: Those about *absolute* size effects and those about *relative size* to other organizations" (Dobrev and Carroll, 2003:543).

Different measures of size are likely to yield different findings, which in turn may lead to inconsistent conclusions. One way or another, organizational size is treated here as a contextual variable; like age, it may serve as a predictor of organizations' mortality. In our view, size per se is not a pathogenic feature that accelerates or delays an organization's death, but a correlate of various hazardous phenomena such as stagnation.

Here are some research findings. Empirical evidence (Freeman, 1982) revealed that in the USA in 1967-1972, half of the large firms failed in just a five-year period. Hannan and Freeman (see Carroll, 1984) compared the *Fortune 500* between 1955 and 1975. Their findings show that less than 54 percent of the organizations remained in the 1975 list in the same form as in 1955 list. Thus, large-scale business organizations are not immune to the likelihood of mortality. Yet, small organizations do have higher rates of failure than large ones (Levinthal, 1991), mainly when the former are also new ventures. Thus, organizational mortality rates decline with size (Hannan and Freeman, 1989). Dobrev and Carroll (2003) conducted a comparative study in four major countries, in which they examined the relationship between the relative size of automobile producers and their mortality rates. They concluded: "The results presented here support the hypothesis that the higher an organization sits on the size distribution, the more it is favored by scale-based selection" (p. 555).

The survival advantage of large organizations over small ones is due to the abundant resources, public legitimacy, and political and economic power of the former as compared with the latter. The strength of large organizations enables them better to absorb and withstand external threats and damages that small organizations are unable to manage due to their weakness. An external *random shock* (such as a political crisis) that would barely scratch the surface of a gigantic organization may completely ruin a tiny one.

As size and age are frequently correlated in the realm of organizations, some research suggests that what seems to be a liability of newness is in fact a liability of smallness. A study of national labor unions in the US disentangled the joint effect of these two variables. The findings led the researchers to the conclusion that the liability of newness was not an artifact of the unions' initial size at the time of their founding (Hannan and Freeman, 1989:256-259). The size of newly established organizations at the first stage of their lives does not account for their mortality or their survival.

Size appears to be co-related with the phenomenon of internal inertia in organizations. Hannan and Freeman (1989:80-90) suggest, "the level of structural inertia increases with size for each form of organization." From their theoretical viewpoint, inertia is judged by organizations' attempts to adjust their structure to changing environmental circumstances. They assume that small organizations are more likely to make structural changes than large ones. But the latter are more likely than the former to be successful in implementing fundamental change in the form of reorganization. This success is presumably due to the capacity of large organizations to cope with external pressures during the transition period from the old structure to the new one. Accordingly, mortality rates decrease with size. Although small organizations tend to implement reorganization, they are apparently too weak to survive this kind of "major surgery." This proposition, however, still requires further empirical substantiation.

In sum, despite various methodological shortcomings, empirical studies generally confirm the "liability of smallness" hypothesis (e.g., Carroll and Hannan, 2000). That is, the probability of death declines as an organization grows in size. The demographic phenomenon is due to several conditions, among them the abundance of unused resources and established connections with clients and suppliers. Apparently, large organizations are likely to resolve internal crises and cope with external pressures. Small organizations are less likely to possess similar buffers, so they face a higher likelihood of mortality in one way or another.

The Niche Factor

It is taken for granted nowadays that organizations' wellbeing and survival depend, to a certain extent, on the conditions of the environments within which they live and function. Organizational environments have long been classified into various types such as "placid," "dynamic," and "turbulent" (Emery and Trist, 1965). Yet, for the study of organizational mortality at least, the concept of environment needs to be more accurately specified. Students of the population-ecology perspective have chosen the concept of *organizational niche* for the purpose of studying organizations' birth and death rates (e.g., Hannan and Freeman, 1989; Hannan, Carroll, and Polos, 2003).

"The niche of a population [of organizations] consists of combinations of resource abundances and constraints in which members can arise and persist" (Ibid., p. 50). Each niche carries one or more populations of organizations of a certain form. An *organization form* is identified by a set of core properties such as stated goals, form of authority, core technology, and marketing strategy (Ibid.). In an attempt to integrate various definitions of the niche concept, Hannan, Carroll, and Polos suggest a set of five criteria by which organizational niches should be identified.

> We build a model of the niche using the following ingredients: (1) a market; (2) an audience with members possessing distinctive tastes; (3) a set of sociodemographic positions associated with the audience members; (4) a set of organizations making offers; and (5) organizations with identities and applicable organizational-form codes. (Hannan, Carroll, and Polos, 2003:312)

Indeed, several empirical studies have applied the concept of organizational niche to voluntary associations, children's daycare centers, investment banks, automobile manufacturers, and semiconductor companies; each study measured the niche by one criterion or another (cf., Hannan, Carroll, and Polos 2003).

Research findings on labor unions obtained by Hannan and Freeman (1989) supported their prediction on the effect of density (i.e., the number of organizations in a population) on mortality rates. As expected, the findings showed a U-shaped, non-monotonic pattern of relationship. In other words, mortality rate, as manifested in the case of labor unions by acts of disbanding, went down as more new unions were founded, until the point where the trend was reversed: the greater the number of unions, the higher the rate of disbanding them. "It is worth emphasizing that estimates of the effects of density are stable and significant even in the presence of strong effects of aging, periods, environmental conditions, and founding conditions" (Ibid., p. 286). Further studies of semiconductors as well as the newspaper industries show similar patterns of non-monotonic relationships between density level and mortality rates. In these three studies, mortality rates fell with the rising number of organizations to a certain point; thereafter, mortality rates inclined upward as the number of organizations kept growing.

The concept of *niche width* refers to the variation of resource utilization by a focal niche (Hannan and Freeman, 1989:104), that is, the extent to which organizations utilize the resource base available in a given niche (e.g., the range of scientific disciplines for which a university confers academic degrees). Organizations are frequently classified as either *specialist organizations* (offering the market one product or a handful of goods or services) or as *generalist organizations* (offering the market a wide variety of goods and/or services). For example, a nursing school represents a specialist type of organization, whereas a department store represents a generalist type. The link between these two concepts is quite clear: specialist organizations narrow the width of the respective niche, and generalist organizations widen it. Hence, "to the extent that larger social trends favor generalist organizations, organizational diversity will decline. But if specialist organizations have adaptive advantages, the society will contain many diverse specialists" (Hannan and Freeman, 1989:310).

Following Carroll's (1985) model of niche width, the chances of survival of generalist and specialist organizations depend on their concentration in the respective market. The likelihood of mortality among specialists goes up when the number of generalists increases in that market. However, if only one or a few generalists dominate the market, the survival chances of the generalists rise and those of the specialists fall.

Finally, demographic studies of restaurants, semiconductor firms, and newspapers publishers (Hannan and Freeman, 1989) regarding the correlation between niche width and mortality rates show that if only one or few generalists dominate the market, the generalists' likelihood of survival rises and that of the specialists declines. In other words, generalist organizations evidently have an overall selection advantage over specialist organizations. But note that under certain conditions of environmental uncertainty the mortality rate of generalist organizations exceeds that of specialist organizations.

The Performance Factor

The concept of *performance* is a key factor in an organization's success or failure. Most scholars and practitioners customarily test an organization's performance in financial terms (e.g., sales volume, profits). No wonder then that an effort has long gone on to identify indicators of performance that may serve as reliable predictors of organizational failure.

For instance, Altman (1983) developed a statistical model of corporate bankruptcy for the United States, known as the Z-Score model, whereby the probability of a given firm going bankrupt can be predicted several years ahead of its actual occurrence. Using Multiple Discriminate Analysis (MDA), this model consists of variables classified into five standard ratio categories: *liquidity, profitability, leverage, solvency, activity.* According to Altman, "the results of our analysis showed impressive evidence that bankruptcy can be predicted as much as two reporting periods prior to the event and that the correct classifications were evident for a sample of firms as well as for original groups of companies" (Altman, 1983:125).

Later, Altman (1983) and his associates developed an improved model, identified as the ZETA model. The model consists of the following seven variables: *return on assets, stability of earnings, debt service, cumulative profitability, liquidity, capitalization, size* (Altman, 1983:132-133). The model proved highly accurate, as 95 percent of the bankruptcies could be predicted one statement prior to the event. The accuracy was quite high, even at five years prior to the actual bankruptcy.

For the last fifty years, several other models aimed at predicting the probable failure of companies have been developed by other scholars (e.g., Wilcox, 1973; Ohlson, 1980; Skogsvik, 2001; Ooghe, 2005). Each of the various models defines the concept of failure somewhat differently from the others.

> In our view the existing management literature which deals with business-failure crises is deficient because: first, most of the contributors to the business failure theory base focus on particular business failure types and contexts without emphasizing their focus explicitly and/or without acknowledging the existence of a range of business failure configurations. (Richardson, 1994)

Hence, the various models utilize different sets of predictors and different statistical/mathematical procedures, and they are likely to arrive at different results (cf. Scott, 1981; Altman, 1983). "At least three distinct types of models have been used to predict bankruptcy: 1) statistical models, primarily, multiple discriminate analyses [MDA], and conditional logit regression analyses, 2) gambler's ruin-mathematical/statistical models, and 3) artificial neural network models" (Jones, 2002).

Just recently, Kumar and Ravi (2007) published a comprehensive review of techniques that have been applied to predict bankruptcy. They categorized them into the following families: (1) statistical techniques, (2) neural networks, (3) case-based reasoning, (4) decision trees, (5) operational research, (6) evolutionary approaches, (7) rough sets, (8) fuzzy logic, and (9) soft computing. The last subsumes seamless hybridization of all the foregoing techniques (see Kumar and Ravi, 2007).

At least some of these models are quite sophisticated, being based on financial ratios, and are difficult to grasp without proper education in the fields of accounting, finances, statistics, or operations research. In recent years, several studies have been devoted to comparisons of the various techniques and their accuracy (e.g., Curram and Mingers, 1994; Dimitras, et al., 1996; Mossman, et al., 1998; Kumar and Ravi, 2007).

The comparisons pinpoint the principal weaknesses of the statistical prediction models. More important, they are criticized for not having an underlying theoretical framework (e.g., Ooghe, et al., 2005). At least some of the models are merely sets of available statistical measures rather than measurement of theoretical concepts. However, the more recently developed and applied models treat organizations as if they were intelligent biological systems, such as human beings: they can be simulated as neural networks, learning processes, decision-making trees, and the like. The later techniques proved more successful than the statistical ones in the prediction of bankruptcies. From their review, Kumar and Ravi (2007) conclude that:

> statistical techniques in stand-alone mode are no longer employed and among the stand-alone intelligent techniques, neural networks were the most often used family, followed by rough sets, CBR [Case Based Reasoning], OR [Operation Research] techniques, evolutionary approaches and other techniques subsuming fuzzy logic, SVM [Support Vector Machine], etc. (Ibid., p. 22)

One way or another, the empirical evidence should lead to the conclusion that failure-prediction models should rely on a combination of several financial measures of performance rather than on a single predictor, accurate as it may be.

Apparently, this kind of failure-prediction model primarily focuses on one mode of failure, bankruptcy. As discussed in the previous chapter, organizational failure may lead to the end of businesses in different ways, of which bankruptcy is only one.

The notion of performance actually blames the organization itself for failure, especially the leadership, whose responsibility it is to ensure its survival. Failure, according to this view, is the outcome of bad management. More concretely, "bad management" means unrealistic strategy, improper decisions, and poor responsiveness to the changing conditions of the organization's external environment. This so-called "bad management" creates serious deficiencies in the organization, adversely affecting its performance and eventually dragging it down to the terminal condition of bankruptcy.

So bankruptcy-prediction models consist of performance indicators that can also serve as warning signals of probable organizational failure. They point to the pressing need of the given organization to induce necessary changes to save itself from collapse. Whether the alarm signals lead to the appropriate actions or not depends largely on the top management.

Conclusion

Organizations, like live organisms, eventually vanish, dispatched by one form of death or another. Organizations are likely to end their existence sooner than later. This chapter dealt with three important factors apparently responsible for organizations' mortality: their age, their size, and the specific niches in which they operate. These, of course, are not the only factors affecting organizations' chances of survival, but they are the most empirically studied in the context of organizations' birth and death rates, therefore, they receive special attention in this volume.

The underlying assumption of this chapter is that an organization's age, size, ownership, type, environmental niche, and similar variables should not, in themselves, be considered direct causes of an organization's chances of survival. They are contextual conditions, in which pathogenic flaws, some fatal, are liable to ripen in organizations. Therefore, they can serve us well as contextual predictors of organizations' mortality rates.

The chapter has presented empirical research findings of rates and patterns of organizational mortality, explained by the factor of age. Three major patterns of mortality rates were identified in these studies: *the liability of newness*, *the liability of adolescence*, and *the liability of senescence*. Each is characterized by a specific trend of organizational mortality that is correlated to an organization's age. The accompanying term "liability" implies certain deficiencies that lessen the chances of survival of organizations of one age or another.

The second contextual factor, organization size, was also discussed in this chapter. Unlike age, size appears to be a rather complex concept since it can be measured in various ways. Some students of organizations, mainly sociologists, prefer to measure size by "head counting," namely, numbering employees, members, clients, or other kinds of contributors. Other scholars refer to size in terms of tangibles: an organization's physical, economic, or financial assets. By whatever means, organizational size may be measured as an absolute or relative parameter.

In general, research findings provide support for the *liability of smallness*. Large organizations are likely to enjoy better survival chances than small. In relative terms, the findings show that the higher an organization's position on the size scale, the greater its likelihood of survival. Still, large organizations are by no means immune, as they have to carry the heavy burden of *inertia*, that is, internal forces that prevent them from changing to adapt to the changing conditions of their environment.

The last contextual predictor addressed in the present chapter was the niche factor. The concept of organizational niche refers to a set of environmental resources in which certain forms of organizations are sustained. Theoretically, as more organizations enter a certain niche—through the founding of new ones—the mortality rate goes down; but only to a certain point, whereupon mortality starts to incline steadily. This change of direction is presumably because the niche becomes too crowded and competition gets tough. Research findings support this hypothesis, showing a U-shape pattern of mortality rates.

A niche may be narrow or wide. Its width affects the mortality rate of organizations, depending on their type. They may be of a generalist or a specialist type. The latter represents organizations that deal with a somewhat limited range of products, whereas the former represents organizations that handle a wide range of products.

The likelihood of mortality among specialists rises when the number of generalists does so; however, if only one or a few generalists dominate the market, their chances of survival rise, and those of specialists decline. Other studies of niche width indicate that generalist organizations are likely to have lower rates of mortality than specialist organizations. Generalists apparently have better survival chances than specialists, except under the specific conditions discussed above in this chapter.

One of the most important predictors of failure and death is the performance factor. Business organizations that perform poorly are more likely to go bankrupt than their comparable good performers. Since the concept of performance is rather complex and somewhat abstract, it has been measured for many years by means of financial/economic indicators. In everyday life, these measures are usually used for periodic evaluation of the worth of businesses.

For over fifty years, scholars have attempted to design and test failure-prediction models that are based on measures of performance. These efforts have produced many formulae which, using various metaphors, are meant to predict bankruptcy of businesses. As the recent models are much more sophisticated than the early statistical ones, they apparently yield more accurate and reliable results. Still, there is neither a single best predictor of bankruptcy nor a unified theory of failure on which such prediction models can rely.

4

Maladies and Disorders

A pathological (abnormal, unhealthy, maladjusted, or inefficient) state in any living system is one in which, for a significant period, either one or more of its critical variables remain beyond the normal steady-state range, or excessively costly adjustment processes must be used to avoid this. (Miller & Miller, 1991:241)

Viewing organizations as natural systems, and using the metaphor of organisms, we can assume that organizations are vulnerable to various pathologies during their life cycle. They appear in the form of malfunctions, disorders, and chronic problems, and in manifestations of misconduct. Like human physical and mental illnesses, these pathologies are sometimes temporary; on the other hand, such deficiencies may take a rather long time, and they are likely to bring about the death of the organization.

Nevertheless, in considering these problems and their consequences, we should not be tempted to equate organizations to human beings. Individuals are always the operators of organizations, but the latter are neither individuals nor merely social groups. We should be at pains to eschew the personification of organizations. The biological analogy is only an analytic tool to better explicate complex phenomena, like pathologies, which are quite difficult to grasp in the context of organizations.

The notion of organizational pathologies implies the existence of grave, life-threatening problems, not some minor discomforts that come and go here and there. In this sense, they resemble physical diseases and mental disorders in human beings. They jeopardize the organization's survival, because they tend to spread to large parts of them and deeply penetrate their culture.

Organizational corruption represents one well-known type of pathology, albeit extreme. Its immoral and illegal nature necessitates perpetual concealment from the public eye. Nevertheless, this pathology tends to be "contagious": it is likely to spread in the organization among senior executives, professionals, and even some lower-level employees. At some point, the corruption is disclosed and it brings about the collapse of the organization, as in the case of Enron Corporation in the U.S. One chapter in this volume is, therefore, wholly devoted to the issue of corruption as one type of organizational pathology. Another organizational pathology that may cause the collapse of organizations and their leaders' imprisonment is so-called "corporate crime." Because of its abnormal nature and far-reaching consequences, this phenomenon, too, merits a chapter of its own in this volume.

As in medicine, *organizational pathologies* may be identified by some observable symptoms. First, they are manifested in organizations in certain distinct patterns, which others perceive as *abnormal* or *deviant* modes of behavior. Second, they harm the organization's participants (e.g., peers) and their outside public (e.g., clients). Third, because they are *self-serving* behavior patterns (e.g., organizational politics) they persist for quite long periods in the organization, and hence might grow worse and pass the point of no return. Fourth, they generate tension and antagonism among the organization's participants—its own sub-units, as well as between the organization and the public. Finally yet importantly, abnormal behavior patterns tend to infect other participants, tainting the entire organization with a stigma such as "bureaucratic," "corrupt," or "anachronistic."

Imagine a college, a hospital, and a bank. For illustrative purposes, assume that all three render their clients somewhat poor service. Since the college teachers are busy moonlighting, they are very slow in marking exams, correcting papers, and providing feedback to their students. At the hospital, the long day and night shifts keep the nurses constantly in a state of being overworked and unable to respond to their patients' urgent needs. The labor cost reduction policy at the bank results in most of its tellers being temporary, part-time employees (e.g., students) positioned there by outsourcing to the Manpower Company. These tellers are not skilled enough to advise the bank's customers on financial matters such as savings, foreign currencies, or loans. So they furnish clients with only minimal, routine-type services (e.g., deposits and withdrawals).

The three organizations, then, display some abnormal patterns of behavior, resulting in low quality services to their customers. In spite of the damage, they make, these deficiencies continue because certain people in the organizations apparently benefit from them in one way or another. As long as these behavior patterns do not create crises, other employees are likely to find ways to do the same thing and perform less, to ease their workload too. At the same time, there might be tensions and conflicts between the good and the bad performers. With the passing of time, these organizations will earn a bad reputation, which will persuade actual and potential clients to keep away. This response by the public may lead eventually to the end of these organizations.

Organizational Deficiencies

Miller and Miller (1991) suggested a classification of the various kinds of deficiencies and shortcomings. It has eight distinctive classes, which the authors identify as "organizational pathologies." Each class represents lack of inputs, excess of inputs, improper inputs, or abnormalities in internal processes. Inputs may be in the form of some solid matter, some kind of energy or another, or inbound and outbound flow of information. For example, one class of pathologies typically refers to a prolonged shortage of raw materials or spare parts; or lack or insufficiency of the energy by which the organization does its work. The pathologies in the next class result from inappropriate material or energy. In these cases, the inputs do not match the organization's equipment or technology. Another class of pathologies contains ongoing absence of information that is necessary for making proper decisions and for good performance of various jobs. The last class of pathologies that we mention here refers to abnormalities in machinery operation, energy consumption, or handling of information. These pathologies are outcomes of serious deficiencies in the *throughput process* by which the organization's goods and services are produced for its clients.

One of the more frequent deficiencies in the realm of organizations is probably a *shortage of working capital*, undoubtedly a critical resource for their survival. It is no wonder that practitioners often call working capital "business oxygen." Organizations ordinarily experience a temporary shortage of sufficient working capital in difficult times, but such problems are usually overcome after a while.

What turns this insufficiency into an organizational pathology is a prolonged period during which the necessary operating funds are nonexistent time after time. This shortage of incoming cash flow makes it difficult for the organization to acquire raw materials, update its equipment, invest in marketing endeavors, and handle current costs.

With such difficulties, an organization is likely to postpone payments to suppliers and subcontractors for their goods and services; to defer wages and salaries to its employees; to take ever-larger loans from the banks; and to accumulate debts. Consequently, the organization drifts to a point of insolvency and, eventually, to its death. It is worth mentioning here that not-for-profit organizations are not immune to this pathological downward path, which may lead them to a state of insolvency, as is briefly related in the following example.

A symphony orchestra of about a hundred musicians had performed a series of classical concerts uninterruptedly for over fifty years. This not-for-profit cultural organization had been supported by annual contributions from the city council of its hometown and by the country's ministry of education and culture. Over one-third of its annual income had come from tickets sold to the public. However, recently the number of subscribers had been gradually declining, and as a result the local and national authorities decreased their annual contributions; moreover, labor costs had gone up with the rising cost of living. Consequently, the orchestra endured a dearth of working capital for three consecutive years. As might be expected, the board of directors decided to withhold part of the musicians' salaries, not to purchase any new instruments, to engage conductors and soloists of a lower level for lower fees than in the past, and to stop paying rent to the owner of the concert hall. However, all these measures proved unable to solve the persistent problem.

The orchestra could neither complete its annual series of concerts nor refund ticket-holders for unperformed concerts. In fact, the orchestra soon became insolvent. All the stakeholders demanded their money back, threatening to take the organization to court. The organization was dissolved, debts were paid, its administrative and support staff lost their jobs, and the musicians got some compensation for the termination of their contracts.

Fortunately, the newly elected mayor of the town had decided to maintain this important cultural asset. The orchestra was re-established as a new public sector enterprise, a new musical leadership was appointed, and some of the musicians took upon themselves administrative tasks. Since then, the orchestra has been improving both its performance as well as its financial condition.

Another pathological deficiency may be designated here as *loss of direction*. This abnormal situation is likely to develop in organizations whose principal values are abandoned due to certain external or internal changes. The displacement of foremost values may impair the functioning of organizations and cause some serious problems. In value-based organizations in particular, such a "loss of direction" can be fatal. By value-based, we mean organizations devoted to the pursuit of religious, educational, medical, cultural, and similar goals. The displacement of traditional values and beliefs in those organizations is likely to encounter resistance by their members and their constituencies alike.

Many public sector organizations subjected to privatization encountered considerable difficulties in reorienting themselves to the values and norms of the private sector. The enforced shift from values of civil service, social contribution, welfare, and helping to values such as efficiency, profitability, competition, and the like proved rather difficult for the members of those organizations. Their transition periods were characterized by internal tensions and disputes, confusion and ambiguity, and low morale. Quite frequently, employees responded with strikes, high turnover, acts of violence, and resistance to necessary changes in their work modes. Little wonder that some of the privatized organizations were unable to endure this pathological state of *anomie* and they met their end after a while.

One of the most interesting cases of loss of direction may be seen in the prolonged crisis of the Kibbutzim (collective communes) in Israel. Starting at the beginning of the twentieth century, the Kibbutz movement established over three hundred agrarian collective settlements all over Israel. They were unique in their strict adherence to egalitarian values, direct participative democracy, their members' self-employment, the accumulation of collective capital and prohibition of private wealth of any kind, and concern for their members' wellbeing.

In addition to intensive agriculture, the Kibbutzim established a range of manufacturing industries, a variety of services, and different kinds of business ventures (Samuel and Heilbrunn, 2001). Over the years, many of them grew and prospered.

For the last twenty-five or so years, Israeli society has undergone considerable changes in values: from humanism to materialism, from collectivism to individualism, and from socialism to neo-liberalism. As a result, the economic regime has changed from a socialistic to a neo-liberalistic system (Samuel and Harpaz, 2004:1-5).

These and other changes of ideas infiltrated the Kibbutzim as well. The displacement of values and goals caused a great deal of confusion, ambivalence, controversy, and high tension among their members for a long period. The entire ideological foundation upon which the Kibbutz movement was built started to crumble. In an attempt to adjust to the new conditions of the surrounding environment, many Kibbutzim wrought changes in their work organizations, in their members' employment, in the rigid norms concerning private income and consumption, and in their socio-economic foundations.

Nevertheless, a considerable number of Kibbutzim suffered economic crises and their members' standard of living declined significantly. Others were compelled to privatize some parts of their collective wealth. Numerous members, mainly the younger and more educated ones, left their communities and their workplaces for good. Some Kibbutzim could not endure the new era and were actually dissolved. The majority of the Kibbutzim are still struggling for their survival, searching for a new ideological direction.

Although the Kibbutz is a unique case in today's society and economy, it demonstrates the importance of an organizational value system for the wellbeing of organizations, as well as the far-reaching implications of a displacement of values for their proper functioning and their life chances. The so-called *loss of direction* here is a pathological situation since its damage to the organization is liable to be serious.

Competition is usually considered beneficial in the realm of business. The benefits of competition are well known to scholars and practitioners, at least as regards business enterprises. However, competition within business firms may prove harmful, even disastrous. Evidently, little has been said about this side of competition in organizations. By the term *detrimental competition,* we refer here to competition between divisions or other subunits that is dysfunctional to the organization as a whole.

This kind of intra-organizational competition becomes pathological when the major sub-units of a large-scale organization compete incessantly for the same stock of resources, such as materials, budgets, clients, or projects. Such competition turns into a so-called zero-sum game within the organization: each unit attempts to increase its own resources at the expense of the other units. Mintzberg (1983) designates this kind of behavior as *suboptimization*: "Each unit, and finally each position, is then expected to pursue its goals to the exclusion of all others. In other words, it is expected to *suboptimize*—to do the best it can on its goals and forget about the rest" (Ibid., p.177).

In no way does this competition enlarge the overall supply available to the entire organization. In fact, these units (divisions, departments) waste precious organizational resources on internal competition, which could be spent on competition with external rivals for the same resources. Worse still, members of these units are likely to manipulate their counterparts in the organization's other units, hiding important information from them and interfering with their work. These and similar counter-productive activities evoke mutual feelings of hostility, blame, denunciation, and alienation. Under such circumstances, organizations are likely to fail sooner or later.

Here is an example of such detrimental competition. A large-scale, high-tech enterprise was structured in multi-divisional form (MDF), with five major divisions concerned with applied research and development of innovative products. Although every division handled different products, they all had a quite similar mix of professional and technical workforce; they used certain multi-purpose laboratories and installations and they worked for the same military market.

As the market started to shrink, these divisions became engaged in ongoing competition among themselves on new R&D projects. In their effort to win clients' bids, each competing division lowered its prices repeatedly, diminishing the potential profits of the organization as a whole. These divisions were not as cooperative as they should have been because of the internal competition. Consequently, they were losing the benefits of internal synergy. They made it very difficult for their professional staff to move from one division to another, so in some divisions scientists and engineers were under-occupied while in others they were overworked.

Internal competition gave rise to various frictions and tensions between divisions, which gradually impaired their own performance as well as that of the organization as a whole. After a while, this kind of debilitating competition becomes an incurable pathology. A similar kind of pathology may be found in academic institutes, in military and police forces, and in government agencies, among others, not necessarily for-profit.

Prolonged hostile relationships between employers and employees are likely to cause deficiencies in an organization's functioning and performance. We will refer to this kind of pathology here as an *industrial unrest*. Its nature is revealed when an organization becomes caught up in series of pernicious labor clashes. As in chronic disease, industrial unrest is characterized by cycles of sudden attacks followed by periods of remission.

Industrial unrest is more likely to evolve in businesses and public services whose employees are unionized. In fact, many of them have several unions since their employees work in different kinds of occupations (e.g., blue collar, grey collar, white collar). In these organizations, the rights and obligations of the two sides are specified in collective agreements, usually negotiated, signed by the union's and the employer's representatives. Nevertheless, in a number of cases, the demands of the parties are too far apart; they become entrenched in rigid positions and the dispute turns into an open struggle.

In such power struggles, employees and employers alike use political tactics such as walkouts, demonstrations, manipulation, lobbying, strikes and shutdowns, and even acts of violence (Samuel, 2005). They create severe problems in the organization's functioning, and they entail serious damage to both parties. More importantly, they also harm customers, suppliers, stockholders, and the public at large, even though the latter are not involved in the dispute. Irregular supply of energy, frequent disruptions of public transport, unreliable means of communication, and mounds of uncollected garbage—these are some well-known examples of the painful consequences of such power struggles.

These harmful situations grow even worse when the attainments of one union spark indignation in the other unions, which demand greater rewards for their members too. This kind of competition between unions leads to a vicious cycle of repeated disturbances in the organization's work. When an unsettling pattern of this kind persists, it becomes a severe pathology, which endangers the organization's survival. The following case study is briefly presented here to illustrate the damage of industrial unrest.

An upscale resort hotel situated near a source of thermal waters, consisting of hundreds of rooms and a well-appointed spa, used to enjoy a worldwide appeal among people with particular health problems (e.g., skin, digestion, nervous tension). At some point, the head office of the hotel's chain realized that, contrary to the past, this particular hotel had been losing money each quarter. An external management consultant conducted an organizational diagnosis of the hotel and found that it had been subjected to an ongoing struggle between its management and the union of that hotel for a considerable period.

The alleged reason for the dispute was the management's preference for hiring a cheap foreign workforce, recruited across the nearby border, instead of employing citizens of its own country, all of them unionized. The foreign employees received much lower wages and poorer fringe benefits than the unionized ones. The hotel's general manager had insisted that the "hiring and firing" of employees was a managerial prerogative in the hotel industry; it was not negotiable under any circumstances.

In support of its members, the union had started a series of sanctions against the hotel's management, such as the shutdown of different services one at a time (e.g., cleaning, maintenance, the spa, the bar, the laundry). In response, the management threatened to withhold service bonuses and discharge employees selectively. Thereupon the union threatened a general strike, which would stop the hotel from conducting business.

As expected, the struggle escalated. What made it even worse was its tendency for the struggle to become ethnic issue between the local and the foreign employees.

Naturally, guests complained of poor service; they cautioned their travel agents abroad not to book any more tourists into that hotel, they refrained from tipping the hotel's staff, and an increasing number of them cut short their stay. In due course, (over a year and a half) the predictable vicious cycle of repeated clashes not only disrupted the hotel functioning and damaged its maintenance and appearance, it ruined its reputation.

Like a malignant disease, this pathological state of affairs deteriorated critically, to the verge of collapse. Only then did all parties involved agree to participate in a turnaround plan that included restructuring and reshuffling the hotel staff. It took the hotel a long and painful time to recover from this traumatic industrial unrest and get back into business.

Abnormal Behavior Patterns

Organization members are likely to be exposed to various kinds of pressures exerted by their clients, supervisors, colleagues, and subordinates. More than a few individuals affiliated to any organization as employees, members, or volunteers are not strong enough to endure such pressures for long. Consequently, some participants walk out of the organization (*exit*); others complain (*voice*), and there are those who respond to such pressures with certain psychological disorders (*neglect*) (Hirschman, 1970).

"A psychological disorder is (1) a psychological dysfunction or dyscontrol within an individual that is (2) associated with distress or impairment in functioning, and (3) a response that is not typically expected" (Barlow and Durant, 2002:25). In the context of organizations, such unexpected responses occur in the form of abnormal behavior of various kinds. Before specifying some of them, it is worth noting here that they tend to be "contagious," and like epidemics, they spread from one individual to other members of the organization.

Workaholism

This well-known habit characterizes individuals who are totally dedicated to their work. A considerable rate of Workaholics may be found in today's high-tech industry in particular. There, large numbers of young, highly educated employees (scientists, engineers, designers, etc.) commonly spend exceptionally long hours in their offices and laboratories. They take their work home on weekends and holidays. They make sure to be in control constantly, wherever they may be, using the most advanced means of communication for that purpose. They frequently go back to their workplace in the middle of the night "just to finish up one assignment or another."

Being so devoted to their work, employees of this kind tend to neglect their family life, avoid social commitments, and refrain from time-consuming leisure activities. Gradually, they turn into "one-dimensional" persons, "willing slaves" to their careers. It is no wonder that workaholics are susceptible to chronic fatigue syndrome (CFS), that is, mental and physical exhaustion or depletion.

At first glance, such dedication to work seems ideal for the employing organizations. In fact, it may prove dysfunctional. Workaholic employees become overloaded with duties and assignments. They have to endure various cross-pressures, handle stressful situations, and maneuver among different assignments requiring their energy, time, and attention. With time their performance declines, hence, their contribution to the organization accordingly. The more participants get addicted to their work, the more grievous the consequences for the organization.

In light of the harmful implications of this pathological trend, an increasing number of clinics and consulting agencies for workaholics serve to help them manage their work-life balance better.

Richard Scott (1992) examines three kinds of problems for individual participants. Since these pathologies are most relevant to our discussion of abnormal behavior patterns, they deserve our attention here. Scott addresses these problems by means of the concepts of alienation, inequity, and over-conformity.

Alienation

This concept has received several interpretations over the years. Broadly stated, alienation refers to a state of detachment between an individual and his or her employment.

> Like Marx, Seeman (1959, 1975) views alienation as a multi-faceted concept; he identifies six varieties: (1) powerlessness—the sense of little control over events; (2) meaninglessness—the sense of incomprehensibility of personal and social events; (3) normlessness—use of socially unapproved means for the achievement of goals; (4) cultural estrangement—rejection commonly held values; (5) self-estrangement—engagement in activities that are not intrinsically rewarding; and (6) social isolation—the sense of exclusion or rejection. (Scott, 1992:321)

All these symptoms are similar to psychological disorders, which are overtly expressed in abnormal behavior patterns such as excessive absenteeism, repeated sicknesses, and minor injuries—likewise, aggressive behavior, lack of involvement in social affairs, and absent-mindedness on the job.

In today's heavily computerized operations and automated work processes, a considerable number of employees do not really grasp the complexities in which their organizations are involved. They have little control of their work and practically no discretion in making decisions concerning their job. Their apathetic approach to customers, their lack of interest in the solution to problems, and the routine mode of doing their work represent symptoms of alienation. In fact, more and more employees are temporary, part-time, and poorly paid; their energy and attention are distracted by activities other than their job (e.g., studies, family affairs, hobbies, moonlighting, alternative careers). Salespersons, waiters, office clerks, receptionists, housekeepers, security guards, and seasonal farm laborers are a few examples of such masses of workers nowadays. Not surprisingly, many of them are alienated from their work and their employers, and their service is mediocre at best.

Inequity

"Formal organizations are expected to be fair in their treatment of personnel: universalistic criteria of hiring, promotion, and pay are purported to operate; achievement is supposed to replace ascription as the basis for distributive rewards" (Scott, 1992:323). Under the concept of inequity, then, employees who make similar inputs receive unequal benefits from their employers in return. Such inequity is quite often the result of deprivation of employees based on their race, gender, ethnic origin, and the like, intended or not. Despite today's laws and regulations, many organizations still tend to be biased in favor of certain social groups so that the other groups have lower chances of enjoying equal opportunities in them.

Organizations that deliberately discriminate against employees on such criteria not only treat them unfairly; they are notorious in the public perception in this respect. Inequity tends to become a real pathological problem of organizations once their stakeholders (e.g., employees, clients) walk out because they are unfair. In such cases, organizations are liable to plummet rapidly. Some political parties, trade unions, and voluntary associations have withered due to the exit of their members and supporters in response to inequity.

Over-Conformity

By this concept, Scott (1992) refers to the tendency of organization members to give preference to rules and procedures over goals and objectives. Mintzberg (1983:177) describes this phenomenon as the inversion of means and ends. This phenomenon of goal displacement resembles a psychological disorder, primarily characterized by unbending adherence to the means of work rather than aiming for the ends that it is supposed to accomplish.

Quite frequently, customers or citizens encounter rigid insistence on the part of an organization's officers and clerks on doing the job only by the book. They agree to render their services if, and only if, the relevant procedure is strictly followed as written. They express their usual excuse by the following cliché: "Sorry Sir/Madam, I don't make the rules, I just follow them." Over-conforming employees tend to ignore the importance and even the critical nature of certain goals (e.g., saving patients' lives, helping needy people to survive, protecting political refugees). They narrowly focus on the means, per se. As Scott claims, "It appears to us that the basis for concern is not the displacement of ends by means but the continued pursuit of means that have somehow become disconnected from, or are at odds with, the ends they were designed to serve" (Ibid., p. 326).

This pattern of pathological over-conformity is liable to become worse under extreme conditions such as crisis or war. Its devastating consequences were revealed after World War II in the German concentration camps in Eastern Europe. The Nazi machine, operated by thousands of German military personnel and local civilians, had succeeded in the systematic genocide of six million Jews and of huge numbers of other ethnic minorities (e.g., Gypsies). This hideous strategy was accomplished only by strict adherence to policies, plans, procedures, and timetables. The executioners would later justify their perpetrating the immense massacre in that they "only followed the instructions of the authorities." Apparently, they performed their appalling task without any application of their own common sense, discretion, or conscience as they directed their helpless victims to their deaths in the gas chambers.

Organizational Neuroses

Another approach to recurrence of problems in organizations is to treat them in psychopathological terms. This perspective presents attempts to explain such problems by an appeal to concepts such as mental disorders (e.g., neuroses). Kets de Vries and Miller (1984:17) explicitly state this outlook: "Just as numerous symptoms combine to indicate a human disorder, similar patterns of strategic and structural defects often point to an integrated organizational pathology." From this point of view, the neurotic personality styles of top executives spread down the lines of command throughout their organizations. Arguably, neurotic styles of top managers are likely to be reflected in dysfunctional behavior of their organizations. Under those circumstances, an individual pathology turns into an organizational pathology.

> We believe that many aspects of strategy, structure, and organizational culture are signifiers (that is, are a function) of the neurotic styles and fantasies of the top echelon of managers. More specifically, the "neurotic" characteristics of executives—the peculiarities of their styles—seem to give rise to uniformities of organizational culture, in the form of myths, stories, and shared beliefs. These are long-lived and self-perpetuating and can, in turn, foster common *organizational* neurotic styles as manifested by certain strategies, structures, and organizational cultures. (Kets de Vries and Miller, 1984:42)

These authors describe five neurotic styles: *paranoid, compulsive, dramatic, depressive,* and *schizoid.*

(1) The Paranoid Organization

This type is characterized primarily by suspicion and mistrust, as well as by hypersensitivity and hyper-alertness. It displays over-concern with hidden motives and maintains intense control and a coldly rational style of behavior.

(2) The Compulsive Organization

This type is characterized by perfectionism. People are preoccupied with tiny details. There is always an emphasis of power distance in interpersonal relationships. It is somewhat dogmatic, stressful, and meticulous.

(3) The Dramatic Organization

This type dramatizes itself, excessively shows emotions, and draws attention to self. It is narcissistic, and is always in pursuit of exciting activities. However, it lacks the capacity for maintaining sharp focus.

(4) The Depressive Organization

This style is expressed by feelings of guilt, worthlessness, self-reproach, and inadequacy. Captured by external control, it expresses a sense of hopelessness and helplessness, hence loss of interest and motivation.

(5) The Schizoid Organization

This neurotic type reflects detachment, noninvolvement withdrawal, and a sense of estrangement. It is also characterized by a lack of excitement, indifference, and lack of interest in the present or the future. It displays a cold, non-emotional appearance.

Kets de Vries and Miller further argue that each of these pathological styles consists of certain organization-wide, deeply rooted problems, manifested in the organization's strategies, structures, and cultures. Since these dysfunctions are mutually reinforcing and pervasive, they are resistant to change.

Conclusion

This chapter has presented a sample of organizational maladies and disorders that tend to be of a pathological nature. These pathologies are neither exhaustive nor exclusive.

The concept of organizational pathology refers to problems that impair organizations' performance, compromise their goals, and endanger their long-term survival. They appear in the form of malfunctions, disorders, recurring problems, and manifestations of misconduct. Their common features serve to classify them as various kinds of "organizational pathologies." Pathologies evolve due to the lack of inputs, excess of inputs, improper inputs, or abnormalities in processing inputs into outputs.

A shortage of critical resources is a severe pathological deficiency. Like breathing difficulties of living organisms that suffer from insufficient oxygen, shortage of working capital has a comparable effect on organizations. Similar pathologies of this kind are a dearth of qualified workforce and up-to-date technology.

Another type of pathology has to do with the purpose and meaning of a given organization. One such pathology is the displacement of values. The transitional period in which a traditional a set of values ceases to be valid and a new set has not yet come into effect represents a loss of direction, or anomie.

Ongoing competition between an organization's divisions and departments elicits conflicts; it also intensifies power struggles between subunits. Such internal competition is likely to be detrimental to the organization as a whole.

Industrial unrest represents a type of organizational disorder character-ized by ongoing clashes between employers and employees. Organiza-tions undergo long periods of instability and unrest, which carry serious implications for their chances of survival.

Organizations also have to bear the consequences of their participants' abnormal behavior patterns. In this chapter, alienation, over-conformity, and inequity were discussed.

Workaholism becomes pathology in an organization when a consid-erable number of employees are addicted to their work. This reaches a point where their chronic fatigue overshadows their work-life balance and throws their job performance into disarray.

Alienation is an expression of employees' detachment from their jobs, their organization, and even their fellow workers. In many cases, it is evinced in frequent absenteeism, a plethora of minor illnesses and injuries, and even walkout.

Over-conformity is excessive emphasis of means at the expense of goals. Over-conforming employees show strict adherence to rules and regulations, forms, and procedures—no matter what.

Feelings of inequality reflect conditions in which certain employees perceive relative deprivation, in terms of income and benefits, simply because they belong to some minority or unprivileged social group.

Organizations are likely to be influenced by their top executives' personalities, disorders, and abnormal styles of behavior. They turn into "neurotic organizations" of different types, characterized by the typical problems.

These and other ailments are likely to hurt organizations because of external or internal factors. Some maladies and disorders may come and go; others may remain for a long time, jeopardizing the organization's chances of survival.

5

The Spiral of Decline

This chapter describes the painful, perilous, and sometimes fatal process of organizational decline that may befall any organization at any time. The decline may be brief and steep, hurtling close to collapse, or prolonged and measured, with the gradual sinking of the organization into infirmity. As discussed in this chapter, declines are liable, but not bound, to terminate in the death of organizations. Some scholars suggest that declines may be reversed, and dying organizations may rise again, like the phoenix (e.g., Guy, 1989). Others scholars (e.g., Hannan and Freeman, 1984) cast doubt onto the feasibility of organizational renewal.

Types of Decline

The concept of *organizational decline* refers to deterioration in the capacity of a certain organization to adapt to the environment within which it is embedded (Greenhalgh, 1983).

> Decline is a two step process in which deteriorating environmental adaptation leads to reduced internal financial resources (Cameron, Sutton, and Whetten, 1988). An organization has environmental support when it has favorable exchange relations with groups and individuals that hold critical resources and when its actions are endorsed by powerful external groups and individuals (see resource dependence). Lost environmental support results from the intertwined deterioration of an organization's image and its resource base. (Sutton, 2005:1)

In other words, "decline is a downward spiraling, in which the organization does enough to survive, but not enough to stop the devolution" (Guy, 1989:6). Whetten further explicates the double meanings of this concept.

> The word *decline* has two principal meanings in the organizational literature. First, it is used to denote a cutback in the size an organization's work, profits, budget, clients, and so forth. In this case, an organization's command over environmental resources has been reduced as a result of either decreased competitive advantage (the organization has a smaller share of the market) or decreased munificence (the total market has shrunk)…The term *decline* is also used to describe the general climate,

or orientation, in an organization. Using the life cycle model, some authors speak of mature organizations that become stagnant, bureaucratic, and passive, as evidenced by their insensitivity to new product developments, workers' interests, and customers' preferences. (Whetten, 1980:345-346)

The first form of decline—cutback—has been taking place recently in numerous organizations, as downsizing in one way or another. The second form—stagnation—lurks everywhere in the world of organizations. This kind of decline resembles the aging of live organisms in nature. Here it is deemed a pathological state of affairs that, if not properly treated, may kill the organization.

Guy (1989) classified decline processes into three major types, which may overlap, as follows: *undiscovered decline, uncontrolled decline,* and *orchestrated decline.* She subdivides the first two into intentional and unintentional types. The former reflect deliberate strategies by management to reduce costs or save other scarce resources such as qualified workers. From the present viewpoint, the unintentional types of decline should be seen as organizational pathologies. They are likely to impair organizations just as diseases debilitate live organisms.

Miller (1977) developed a typology of business failure syndromes, which includes four major types. "Failure…means protracted periods of poor profits and eroding market share but not necessarily bankruptcy" (Miller, 1977:43). This definition of failure is similar to that of decline, as used here, at least in business organizations. Let us glance briefly at Miller's typical syndromes.

Type 1: The Running Blind

Firms of this type fail because power-thirsty chief executives, who set unrealistic goals and over-ambitious strategies, dominate them. Such firms are highly centralized, over-diversified, and devoid of clear long-term plans, and their uncontrolled growth does not match their resources.

Type 2: The Stagnant Bureaucracy

This type of organization is not responsive to new needs of the external environment. Such organizations resist the implementation of necessary changes; they rely on their past successful strategies; and they emphasize rules and procedures in a highly bureaucratic manner.

Type 3: The Headless Firm

Large firms of this type are highly diversified and decentralized. Top management barely controls the strategies, operations, and performance

Figure 5.1
Types of Decline

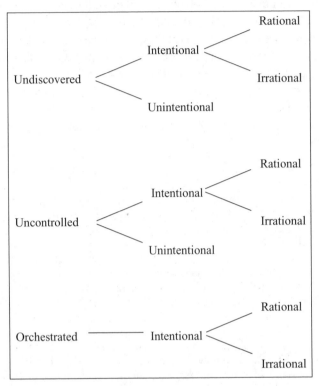

of the major units. Leadership is weak, strategy vague, and performance low. These firms suffer uncoordinated strategies and hazy direction.

Type 4: The Aftermath

Business firms of this type have endured sundry difficulties and a variety of failures in the past. They suffer from a shortage of resources, old technologies, and mismanagement. Often, new executives with limited experience in the particular industry, who make wrong decisions and fail in their attempts to turn the grave situation around, lead them. They teeter on the edge of bankruptcy and, in fact, are more likely to collapse than the other types.

The Downward Spiral

Organizational decline has been described in the literature as a downward spiral, whereby the organization sinks ever deeper (e.g., Forrester, 1971; Bozeman and Slusher, 1979; Staw, Sandelands, and Datton, 1981). In this process, each stage is more serious than the last, leading to its inevitable end. Three models of such a downward spiral deserve attention here, since they clarify, each from a different viewpoint, the pathological nature of this process.

Mary Guy (1989) depicts the downward spiral as a sequence of eight stages:

1. *Recognition.* Executives ignore signs of trouble and danger signals, dismissing them merely as exceptional events.
2. *Stress.* Recognition of the situation creates stress due to premonition of forthcoming crisis. Stress negatively affects the quality of decisions in the organization, leading to serious mistakes, which heightens the feelings of stress.
3. *Circle the wagons.* In the face of crises, executives form a tight circle within which they exchange information with those who are in agreement with them. Hence, they focus on minor issues, attempting to make some minor changes that are not liable to halt the declining process.
4. *Restricted information flaw.* "Decision makers go into a crisis mode, fall back on the routines they know best, and do not seek or attend to information that is contrary to their own beliefs and opinions" (ibid., p. 43). Least of all they listen to the ideas of subordinates, who know first hand what the problems are and how they should be handled.
5. *Finger pointing.* Feelings of guilt and remorse lead to the diffusion of gossip and rumors through which they attribute blame to others. As a result, members of the organization, distrusting one another, are busy dispelling the rumors and the gossip at the expense of their own work.
6. *Collective rationalization.* Managers and other groups of decision makers develop beliefs that they avail of whatever is needed to prevent crisis. They collectively hold to certain explanations as to why and how they have behaved rationally and responsibly all the way. Those who disagree with or disavow such accounts are excluded from the group as dissidents.
7. *Defective decision making.* In an attempt to resolve the crisis quickly, decisions are made based on limited information, improper consideration of alternatives, and shortsighted vision. Consequently, an unsuitable remedy in the form of some strategic or structural change is liable to be imposed on the organization.
8. *Continued decline.* The sequence of all these stages exerts increasing pressure on the declining organization. The spiral of decline continues to plunge deeper and deeper, to the point of no return. The inability of

an organization to halt the decline right at the beginning by appropriate measures may well result in its death. The longer the process of descent, so is the process of the ascent, if is possible at all. Eventually, such organizations may not be able to renew their past vitality, and they are doomed to pass away.

According to Weitzel and Jonsson (1989), decline occurs because of an organization's inability to discern alarm signals. "Organizations enter the state of decline when they fail to anticipate, recognize, avoid, neutralize, or adapt to external or internal pressures that threaten the organization's long-term survival" (ibid., p. 95). Once the decline has started, it can easily turn into a slide down to the organization's dissolution.

Following the analogy used here, decline resembles a prolonged pathological illness, which is liable to develop due to negligence or denial on the part of the sick patient. Addicts to various substances may serve

Figure 5.2
Widening Performance Gap as Decline Deepens

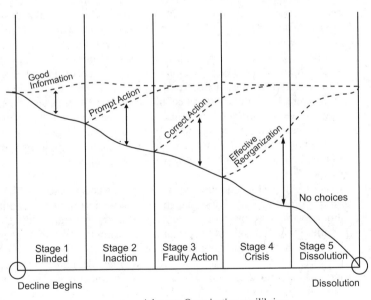

Source: Reprinted from "Decline in Organizations: A Literature Integration and Extension," by William Weitzel and Ellen Jonsson, published in *Administrative Science Quarterly*, Volume 34(1), pp. 91-109, by permission of ASQ. Copyright © Johnson Graduate School of Management, Cornell University.

as good examples of such unresponsiveness to external and/or internal health threatening signals. Their failure to pay careful attention to early symptoms leads to an inevitable process of physical deterioration, which most probably will end in their early death.

Based on their conceptualization of decline, Weizel and Jonsson (1989) went a step farther and developed a five-stage model of organizational decline, which they portray as a downward spiral.

1. *Blinded.* At this first stage of decline, organizations do not detect environmental changes or internal symptoms that threaten their long-term survival. Organizations, like human beings, have blind spots. Nevertheless, the ones leading to decline (and eventual demise) are too serious to be left unattended. Shrinkage of the target market, a growing demand for alternative products, and a relocation of investment funds to other business areas are only a few examples of such external changes. Unfit organizational structure, an overly large workforce, and congested communication channels are typical symptoms of such unnoticed changes in organizations.

2. *Inaction.* The second stage is characterized by lack of appropriate action by management to the downward slide. Executives tend to postpone corrective action, since this usually involves implementation of necessary change. They fear to admit failure; they are hesitant to diverge from the well-known course into a different and uncertain direction; they like to believe that the developing crisis is just temporary; and they trust in the strength of the organization to survive all sorts of difficulties.

3. *Faulty Action.* At this advanced stage of decline, making correct decisions and taking proper steps becomes critical. Instead, executives are likely to vie for shrinking resources, form coalitions and oppositions, and initiate actions that are ineffective at this stage. Even if top management eventually does make the right decisions (e.g., turnaround), implementation encounters many obstacles to embarking on the correct course.

4. *Crisis.* At this stage, the deterioration process gets worse, and the declining organization is barely capable of solving its problems. Conflicts among various groups worsen. Feelings of anger, frustration, guilt, and blame spread throughout the organization. Clients look for alternative products made by other organizations; investors are more reluctant to pour money into the organization, and suppliers demand tighter credit terms. Under these circumstances, it becomes imperative to reorganize effectively; the alternative is entry into the final stage of decline.

5. *Dissolution.* This is the last stage of decline—indeed the end of the given organization's life. The costs of maintaining it soar ever higher. The leadership has too few resources and too little experience to handle such a grave situation. The choice is to sellout, declare bankruptcy, or dissolve. One way or another, this situation takes the decline irreversibly to its end.

Hambrick and D'Aveni (1988) developed a third model that portrays organizational decline as a downward spiral. These authors based their model on an empirical study in which they compared matched samples of large business firms that went bankrupt between 1972 and 1982 with firms that were not bankrupted in the same period. The two samples (fifty-three pairs of large companies) were compared in four major constructs related to failure by various scholars before their study. These were the firm's domain (product/market) initiatives, the environmental capacity to support the organization, the firm's uncommitted resources, and its level of profitability. Their downward spiral model consists of four main phases, as graphically depicted in Figure 5.3.

1. *Origins of Disadvantage.* This is the early stage, in which the seeds of weakness are sown. The firms that later on are bankrupted already lag behind the surviving firms in their levels of slack resources and profitability.
2. *Early Impairment.* The relatively low levels of slack resources and profitability further deteriorate from viable to marginal.
3. *Marginal Existence.* The failing firms adopt extreme strategies such as inaction or hyper-action; they veer from one strategy to the next. Their working capital is similar to that of the survivors and their environment's capacity to carry them is neutral.
4. *Death Struggle.* This last stage sharply lowers the survival chances of the failing firms. Their slack resources severely decline, as does their performance. Their environment significantly shrinks and they continue to swerve from one strategic direction to another. Those failing firms are doomed to die.

Origins of Decline

Decline is the outcome of certain factors operating inside as well as outside the organization, so two major origins of organizational decline and death represent these origins. The first resides within the organization itself, designated as *r-extinction*; the second one resides in the organization's environment, identified as *k-extinction*. The latter refers mainly to the organization's niche. Every niche has a limited capacity to carry a certain quantity of organizations. The upper limit, K, indicates the maximal number of organizations that a given niche can support at any time. "Organizations that decline short of the upper limit are generally victims of poor management (*r-extinction*)." Their failure to remain competitive is self-induced. "In contrast, organizations that decline at the zenith of the carrying capacity curve are victims of a depleted resource pool (*k-extinction*)" (Whetten, 1987:348).

Figure 5.3
Organizational Decline as Downward Spiral

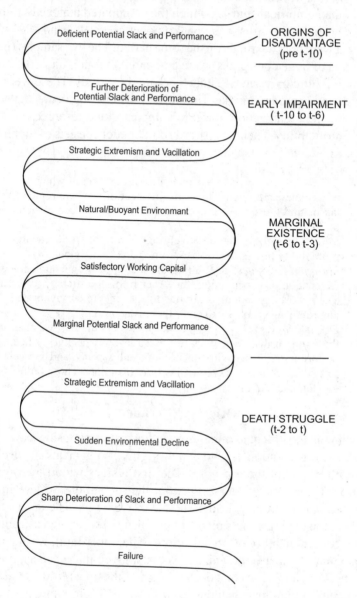

Deficient Potential Slack and Performance — ORIGINS OF DISADVANTAGE (pre t-10)

Further Deterioration of Potential Slack and Performance — EARLY IMPAIRMENT (t-10 to t-6)

Strategic Extremism and Vacillation

Natural/Buoyant Environmant — MARGINAL EXISTENCE (t-6 to t-3)

Satisfectory Working Capital

Marginal Potential Slack and Performance

Strategic Extremism and Vacillation

Sudden Environmental Decline — DEATH STRUGGLE (t-2 to t)

Sharp Deterioration of Slack and Performance

Failure

Source: Reprinted from "Large Corporate Failures as Downward Spiral", by Donald C. Hambrick and Richard A. D'Aveni, Administrative Science Quarterly, Volume 33, pp. 1-23, March 1989, by permission of ASQ. Copyright © Johnson Graduate School of Management, Cornell University.

Based on Levine's (1978) typology of the causes of crisis in the public sector, Whetten (1980:354-362) modified it to include business organizations in the private sector too. This typology of the origins of organizational decline is worth noting here.

Organizational Atrophy

A decline process, in this case, reflects the "success breeds failure" syndrome. Organizations decline because of their inability to respond properly and in good time to changes in their environment. Their executives and mangers rely on past success as an assurance of future success. External threats developing in their environment are overlooked or underestimated. Instead of implementing new policies and programs, decision makers insist on doing the same things in the same ways as in the past. Such organizations become constrained by inertial forces, hence non-adaptive to their external conditions. These are signs of disorientation, or senility, which drive the organizations down into decline and lead to death.

Vulnerability

This source of organizations' decline lays weaknesses that make them more vulnerable than others to failure and demise. Decline in this case reflects the "failure breeds further failure" syndrome. As repeatedly shown by various ecological studies (discussed here earlier), organizations are more vulnerable or less according to their age. The best example of such a state of vulnerability is probably the incapacity of infant organizations to cope with the demands and pressures of the environment, a state named by Stinchcombe (1965) "the liability of newness." But note that although liabilities of age may initiate prolonged processes of decline, they may also bring about to the sudden collapse of organizations.

Loss of Legitimacy

Organizations of most kinds need legitimacy to survive. Legitimacy brings in funds, investments, clientele, and favorable public opinion. Organizations in the public sector, like state agencies, are more dependent on legitimacy than other kinds of organizations. These in particular make continuous efforts to cultivate political ties and win the support of decision makers in the circles of power. Legitimacy is an important resource whereby organizations can fend off attempts to shut them down on grounds of inefficiency or obsolescence. Accordingly, loss of legitimacy is a source of decline and a threat to survival.

Environmental Entropy

Organizations need to be sustained by their task environment, namely, their specific niche in which they conduct their particular business. As discussed in detail in another chapter, the relevant environment in general and the niche in particular are a source of organizational decline. Once the environment starts to erode, shrink, or fill up densely with competitors some organizations begin their fall. To avert the danger organizations can downsize or exit that niche. The literature suggests that such strategies may salvage the declining organization from an even steeper plunge, whereas denial and inaction are liable to bring such organizations to their end.

From a life-cycle viewpoint, organizational decline is by no means a random event or just bad luck. Like a major disease or mental disorder, decline is a pathological course, rooted in the biography of the focal organization. By the medical and/or psychological analogy, the likelihood of decline is a combination of the organization's form and the nature of the environment to which it is exposed. The former affects its disposition to stagnate at some point of time; the latter stimulates the situational conditions that bring about the pathological state of decline.

In this context "organizational form" consists of the organization's features such as age, size, ownership, location, etc., its structural configuration, its culture and principal values, its type of leadership and quality of management, and so forth. "Organizational environment" refers to the relevant features of the organization's environment such as its complexity, its stability, its level of uncertainty, the abundance of its resources, and so on.

Symptoms of Decline

Their participants—employees, members, or others—who maintain and operate them, populate organizations of all kinds. These are usually the first to notice that their organization is in decline. Once the dangers of decline are perceived by the participants, mainly the rank-and-file, a series of reactions puncture the organization through and through. They are likely to take the form of negative emotions and counter-productive acts. They themselves may therefore be regarded as symptoms of organizational decline. Let us consider some of them.

Low Morale

Naturally, individuals who suddenly realize that their workplace is in trouble, and may collapse, suffer depressive feelings—typically anxiety, fear, despair, and vulnerability. The morale of weak employees with nothing to gain and everything to lose sinks even lower than that of the stronger participants, like managers and professionals. Low morale can characterize not only work organizations; it may also oppress members of a declining trade union, political party, sports club, or voluntary association. An acute observer will discern an aura of sadness overlying participants in any organization under decline.

High Stress

The prospect of closure of an organization to which people are affiliated naturally elicits high stress as well. Their day-to-day behavior reflects it: participants display gestures of impatience and impoliteness, which they cannot hide, to their clients. They frequently argue with their superiors about various work matters; minor conflicts between peers are much more prevalent than before; supervisors tend to be rude to subordinates; and incidents of verbal and even physical violence occur here and there in the organization.

High Turnover

Declining organizations suffer relatively high exit rates of their members. In businesses, many of them are victims of layoff. The more competent employees and those with professional connections outside the organization are the first to quit the sinking workplace for jobs elsewhere. In high-tech enterprises such exits swell into a "brain drain," since they take with them expertise and classified information that legally belong to the organization. In response, declining organizations search for temporary part-time workers provided by external workforce suppliers to fill some of the gaps until the advent of better times. At a time of decline, employees are also shunted from their regular job to others in different divisions or departments in the organization, sometimes in remote places. This policy is more typical of the public sector, where "hire and fire" policy is very difficult to realize.

Low Productivity

Rumors, speculation, and discussion occupy much of the employees' time, attention, and energy at a time of decline. The less the management furnishes official information, the more employees tend to rely on hearsay. Not surprisingly, workers, mainly those on the production lines, spend more time talking than doing their job. Where the employees are unionized, they attend meetings called by the union; they take part in demonstrations, in work sanctions, and in short strikes. On the job, a good many of them evaluate the situation like this, "This workplace is going down, so why should I bother?"

Many Accidents

In light of all these pressures, the rate of accident and injury is likely to exceed normal. Employees become more absent-minded, less careful, do no conform to the required safety precautions, and behave more recklessly. Some workers consume more alcohol and tobacco, others take tranquilizer pills, and some even resort to one kind of drug or another. Substances of this kind are liable to have an adverse effect on workers' judgment on the job, exposing them to greater mental pressures and higher physical risks.

Obviously, the longer and deeper the process of decline, the more intense these symptoms are among members of the sinking organization. Under these circumstances, top management encounters greater difficulties in its attempt to halt the downward trend and turn it around. The more the symptoms spread through the organization the less likely its members are to cooperate with a management in whose competence they no longer trust. The effects of an organization's decline on its members may prove to hasten its death.

Responses to Decline

Organizations tend to respond to processes of decline in different ways. Some organizations attempt to cope with their declination by becoming more rigid (e.g., Staw, et al., 1981).

> This model maintains that threats to organizations are followed by rigid responses such as restriction of information, constriction of control and emphasis on efficiency. Generally, rigidity reflects the tendency towards well-learned or dominant responses, and failure to alter such responses on the face environmental change. (Rosenblatt and Mannheim, 1996:954)

The alternative model maintains that decline presents an opportunity for change and renewal. Declining organizations that face crises are likely to make the necessary effort to cope with environmental pressures by the application of new routines and by means of structures that are more flexible (e.g., Cyert and March, 1963).

Kim Cameron and his associates (1987) examined the responses of American colleges to their decline. They made a distinction between top-management responses and members' responses to decline as well as to turbulence. The former refer to responses such as centralization, no long-term planning, nonselective cuts, and turnover. They indicate the tendency of top-management to adopt a set of rather rigid reactions to the threats of decline or turbulence. The latter refer to responses such as scapegoats, resistance to change, fragmented pluralism, low morale, lost of leader credibility, conflict, and no innovation. These responses also indicate the extent to which an organization's members display rigidity in the face of decline or turbulence. The results of that study reveal a quite complex picture, which shows that top-management responds differently than organization members to the threats of decline. Largely, this study furnished some support to the *threat-rigidity* thesis.

On the other hand, "there is a body of research that suggests just the opposite conclusion—organizational decline may function as a stimulus for adaptation. "This could be described as the 'necessity is the mother of invention' perspective" (McKinley, 1993:4). The studies of Miles and Cameron (1982), McKinley (1984), and Koberg (1987) present a few examples that furnish support to this claim.

Rosenblatt and Mannheim (1996) conducted an empirical study of responses of management to decline. Their research covered the entire electronics industry of Israel. To determine the extent to which organizations had responded to their decline in a rigid or flexible pattern, four responses were chosen (i.e., administrative intensity; workforce cutback; organizational politics; and downward communication). The findings of the study reveal that, "the level of rigidity is far from being uniform both across organizations and across functions" (Ibid., p. 979). Apparently, the terms "rigidity" and "flexibility" do not represent polar ends of the same variable.

Evidently, the response of organizations to the process of decline displays itself in various forms that do not necessarily align toward the same direction. Thus, declining organizations tend to respond both rigidly and flexibly at the same time. Mixed reactions, as such, reflect the confusion and anxiety that the managers and the members of those organizations feel in the face of severe threat to their organizations' survival. Once again, such feelings and responses resemble those of dying human beings.

Recovery and Renewal

As already stated, decline does not necessarily terminate in the death of the organization. Like individuals who suffer from some prolonged physical or mental problems, organizations too may interrupt their sinking at some point, and start to rise again. This change of direction is designated in the literature as *turnaround* or *renewal*. "A central question in research has been the examination of why and how some organizations are able, and others are not, to begin a turnaround in a crisis situation and make it succeed" (Lamberg and Pajunen, 2005:950).

Turnaround is not a one-time incident but a process of gradual recovery, which, in some cases, may be quite prolonged. Mary Guy nicely describes this process using an ascending-the-staircase analogy:

> Although the end results are different, organizational resurrection and organizational decline are similar in their progression. Both occur in stages and each stage builds on the foundation provided by the prior stage. The resurrection process is characterized by a series of steps resembling an ascending staircase. Each step up represents a new phase grounded in the prior phase. Between each step, there is a plateau. (Guy, 1989:98)

One model (Bibeault, 1982) divides the process of turnaround into stages: change of management, evaluation of the situation, state of emergency, stabilization, and back to normal growth. In the first stage, it is necessary to grasp the seriousness of the problems that are pulling the organization down and to replace the leadership that has been responsible for them. The essential second stage is an analysis of the organization's strengths and weaknesses by the new leader. The nature of the major problems, and the extent they endanger the organization's survival, must be identified. In the third stage, an action plan is designed and implemented to staunch the financial bleeding. This is a traumatic stage (like surgery) in which costs are cut, workforce is reduced, and activities are terminated as quickly as possible. The fourth stage consists of efforts to stabilize the organization and to make future plans. This is a settling-down process. The last stage concentrates on development of the company: new investment, new products, new markets, more sales, improved customer services, and higher revenues.

Another turnaround model describes this process of rising through four major stages (Chowdhury, 2002).

1. *Decline*: the series of events that diminish the level of resources of the organization and lower its level of performance;
2. *Response initiation*: the strategies and operations launched by the declining organization in order to rise again;
3. *Transition*: the longest stage, the period in which the fruits of the efforts made in the previous stage gradually start to ripen;
4. *Outcome*: the turnaround process needs to be brought to a conclusion, when it is revealed whether it has succeeded or not. Measures of performance are applied and their findings are assessed.

Figure 5.4
The Turnaround Process

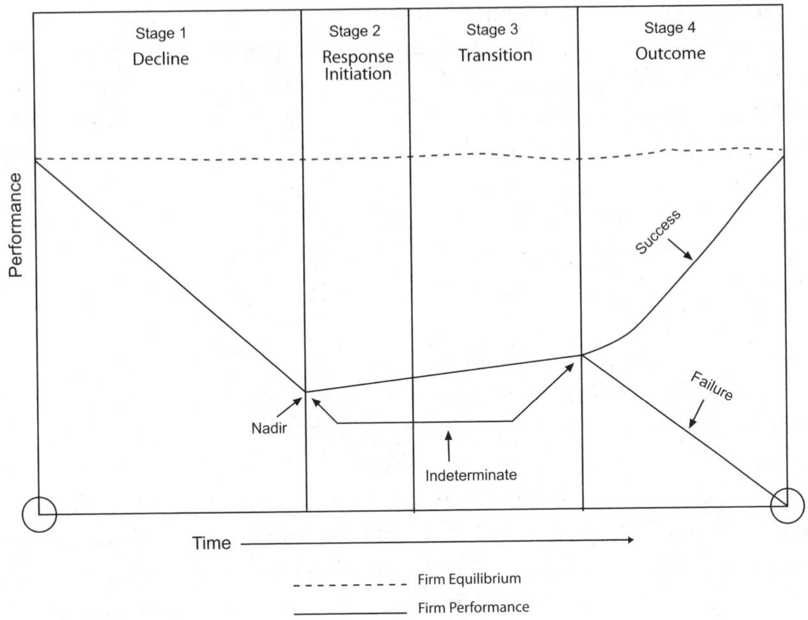

The vertical scales on this gure are purely illustrative. In fact, it is difficult to develop accurate interval scales * for all four stages of turnaround as their duration varies.

Source: Reproduced from "Turnarounds: A stage Theory Perspective", by S. D. Chowdhury. *Canadian Journal of Administrative Sciences*, 19, 3: 249-266., by permission of ASAC © 2002 and the author.

Evidently, the decline and turnaround processes both consist of similar features; this is because the two are, in fact, a collective response to existence-threatening crises (Lamberg and Pajunen, 2005). However, contrary to the downward process, elevation of the organization demands the application of enormous energy.

Briefly, the concept of *Turnaround* refers to the recovery of an organization following a state of decline (Hofer, 1980; Pearce and Robbins, 1993; Barker and Duhaime, 1997; Lamberg and Pajunen, 2005). Such a recovery is likely to succeed if the organization's members are willing to launch such a difficult project, despite its prospective costs and risks.

It is from the literature that, as its name implies, turnaround management involves taking an organization that has been buffeted by vagaries of diminished resources and setting it upon a new course. With rare exceptions, organizations are turned around only after the internal organizational and personal consequences of decline are so pervasive and severe that a consensus has grudgingly emerged. (Whetten, 1987:345)

Several successful turnaround strategies based on the assumption that organizations decline due to their incompetent managements are to be found in the literature (e.g., Argenti, 1976; Hofer, 1980; Bibeault, 1982; Hambrick and Schecter, 1983; Zammuto and Cameron, 1985; Guy, 1989). In case studies, Hofer (1980) identified the following four main turnaround strategies that had proved successful: (1) *asset reduction*, (2) *cost cutting*, (3) *revenue generation*, and (4) *product/market refocusing*. Declining businesses tend to pursue any of these strategies depending on their position at the time of decline, that is, how deep the decline has gone.

Hambrick and Schecter (1983) studied 260 businesses that had experienced decline; later some succeeded in making an improvement while others failed to do so. These authors identified three major successful turnaround strategies applied by declining organizations: (1) *asset/cost surgery* cuts costs by cutting down on research and development, marketing, inventories, along with reducing assets such as plant equipment and new technologies. (2) *Selective product/market pruning* consist of raising direct costs, prices, and product quality to attain a leading position in specific niches. This strategy also includes decreasing marketing and inventory expenses, narrowing the variety of product-lines, and greater labor productivity aiming to shift the focus to the organization's product and market. (3) *Piecemeal strategy* focuses on a few moves gradually intended to increase the organization's capacity utilization (i.e., climb above breakeven point), improve employee productivity, and maintain a high market share.

Other successful turnaround strategies were identified by Miles and Cameron (1982) and by Zammuto and Cameron (1985). Based on the former authors' typology of business strategies, the latter authors suggested five modes of successful response to a state of organizational decline. (1) *Domain defense* focuses mainly on preservation of the organization's domain activities when challenged by hostile pressure from the environment. As in the case of the tobacco industry in the United States, these pressures are manifested mainly by political threats and efforts at de-legitimatization. One way to counter them is coalition formation among competing organizations at the industry level. (2) *Domain offense* is primarily a means of expanding the organization's domain. This aggressive strategy is a response to economic pressures and threats from competitors and other rivals in the product-market domain. Two strategies proved successful in this context: product innovation and market segmentation. The first aims to introduce better products, the second to tailor the market to meet the different preferences of the potential clientele. (3) *Domain creation* attempts to diversify the variety of products and markets. A strategy of domestic diversification and expansion to new markets abroad is likely to be a successful domain creation. (4) *Domain consolidation* narrows the organization's domain by utilizing its core products and/or services. Strategies of this type aim to differentiate the focal organization from its competitors by specializing in a limited range of range of products with which it is identified in the market. (5) *Domain substitution* is a kind of goal displacement. In practice, strategies of this type attempt to replace the organization's initial activities with new ones, most likely in the same area of specialty. Such a replacement may save the organization from imminent demise by making it useful once again for the real needs of the present-day market.

One important limitation of the foregoing turnaround strategies, and of others, is their concentration on declining business enterprises. Naturally, turnarounds are scrutinized through financial lenses, and their outcomes are assessed in terms of profits. But not-for-profit organizations decline too, and their existence may also be at risk. Educational, medical, and welfare organizations and the like are liable to fail because of poor performance or a changing environment, sometimes both. They too need various remedies to salvage them before it becomes impossible to do so. Still, public sector organizations are difficult to measure in terms of performance, and for them the meaning of turnaround is somewhat more ambiguous (cf., Paton and Mordaunt, 2004).

> The turnaround problem in public organizations is more complex than in a business environment. Traditionally, the key difference between poorly performing business and public sector organizations has been understood in terms of the risk of closure or takeover faced by the former because of market pressures, hence easing the turnaround process, while the latter may continue indefinitely because of the greater difficulty in measuring performance and the more diffuse political imperatives to which they are subject. (Jas and Skelcher, 2005:196)

However, in the present era of deregulation and massive privatization of public services the probability of an organization in the public sector, dying is much higher than it was in the past. Governments of many countries prefer to sell off state-owned organizational bodies and hand over their management to private owners. Large-scale public organizations, such as defense industries, national airlines, railways, postal services, and seaport authorities, have been sold to private investors. Other service organizations have been merged with larger and stronger ones in the public sector; some public organizations (e.g., schools, hospitals) have been closed for good, and their premises redesigned to serve other purposes (e.g., museums).

These constraints notwithstanding, waning non-profit organizations in the public sector everywhere make a serious effort to turn around and recover from a state of prolonged failure. They must absorb relevant lessons in the business sector. These lessons were summarized by Paton and Mordaunt (2004:210).

> Successful turnarounds are characterized by "twin track" interventions and behavior. More specifically, reorganizations combining "old blood" (especially in operational areas) with "new blood" (more often in finance and marketing). Combining "negative" approaches (cutting back, closing cherished projects, selling off) with "positive" approaches (investment, risk-taking, enthusiasm for new opportunities). Centralizing most else—to preserve resources while maximizing involvement. Displaying a "bias for action" with a focus on implementation (to end prevarication and demonstrate that change is happening), while seeking and pursuing a consistent, strategic orientation.

Conclusion

Organizations, like other organisms, go through periods in which they expand and periods in which they shrink during their life cycle. This chapter dealt with the issue of shrinkage, known as "organizational decline." The notion of decline refers to a downward trend through which organizations gradually lose their resource base, so they tend to collapse, or at least remain in a poor condition for a prolonged time. In many cases, decline processes end in the death of the organization, in one form or another. This process of descent resembles processes of progressive diseases or mental disorders in human beings, which may be terminal. Therefore, organizational decline is here regarded as pathological processes of various types, which may or may not turn around.

The dynamics of decline processes has been portrayed in stages, dropping from one stage to the next, each lower and deeper than the preceding. Since organizational decline is a downward progression, it may best be described as spiral deterioration.

Decline processes are triggered by two major sources: internal factors in an organization itself (identified as *r-extinction)* and changes in an organization's external environment (identified as *k-extinction*). Decline characterized by the former is likely to evolve because of incompetent management, inertial forces, and inappropriate strategies.

Decline characterized by the latter tends to occur through diffusion of novel technologies, dissemination of new products, and a change in the preferences of the market or the public served, each of which erode the niche where the focal organization operates.

Members of declining organizations often develop harsh feelings (e.g., anger) and counter-productive modes of behavior (e.g., exit) in response to this threatening situation. Such emotional and behavioral responses are typical symptoms of this unhealthy state of affairs. The likelihood of the organization's closure intensifies accusations against the management, enhances fears and anxieties of possible job losses, and encourages flight from the failing concern. Ironically, these and similar symptoms may themselves prove detrimental to its future survival.

Not all decline processes are bound to kill the organization. Executives are often able to lead a new phase of recovery. Efforts at revival are known in the literature as turnaround attempts. Like the decline, any turnaround is also likely to be prolonged, costly, and difficult to accomplish. Accordingly, turnarounds progress in connected stages as well. Each stage advances the organization to a turning point, where it starts to rise. When the organization has stabilized itself as a healthy and vital entity, business can resume as usual. Still, despite this optimistic outlook, a long and deep decline is difficult to turn around.

6

The Perils of Politics

In this chapter, we will consider the issue of politics in organizations, as seen from the viewpoint of organizational pathology. Scholars and practitioners recognize the presence of politics in all kinds of organizations (e.g., Bacharach and Lawler, 1980; Pfeffer, 1981; Samuel, 2005; Clegg, Courpasson, and Philips, 2006; Fleming and Spicer, 2007). "To be blunt, power and politics are endemic in organizations" (Fleming and Spicer, 2007:11). However, only a few scholars have paid close attention to the dangers of the effect of politics to the wellbeing and even the very survival of organizations (e.g., Mintzberg, 1983). Although politics is an integral part of organizational life everywhere and, despite its potential benefits, under certain conditions it may become a detrimental factor.

To understand under what circumstances and in what ways organizational politics changes from a normal to an abnormal facet of organizations it is necessary to explicate this concept briefly here.

The Nature of Politics

Politics rests primarily on the mechanism of power: power plays the same role in politics that money plays in economics. Power in social relationships serves as the driving force that enables some actors (individuals, groups, or organizations) to realize their preferences and attain their goals despite the resistance of other actors; social power is coercive in nature (Weber, 1947). The power of one actor over another depends on the resources available to the former relative to those available to the latter, that is, the extent to which an organizational actor is able to influence others by managing valuable resources that enable him or her to promise rewards or to threaten penalties. "Power in the present sense means control over rewards and/or penalties that give one actor, A, the capacity to induce otherwise unwilling compliance by a second actor, B" (Samuel and Zelditch, 1989:288).

Given the hierarchical nature of organizations, their participants obviously possess different amounts of authority, but also of power. No wonder then that the more powerful participants tend to exercise their power over the less powerful to realize their preferences. Such uses of power reveal themselves in various political acts that those in power positions (e.g., executives, managers, supervisors) operate against the less powerful persons in the organization.

> The term *organizational politics* means any use of power to obtain a desired outcome, including the actual or promised application of rewards and penalties in certain relationships that coexist between different actors who are involved in the organizational activity. (Samuel, 2005: 45-46; see also Gunn and Chen, 2006)

According to this line of thought, political behavior of participants may take various forms, such as persuasion, manipulation, deception, seduction, coercion, and so forth.

Thus, the term *organizational politics* does not usually refer to the exercise of authority, to the enforcement of the law or the rules of the organization, or to decisions by executives aimed at advancing the organization's goals and strategies. Instead, organizational politics consists of actions and interactions that are self-serving, power-based types of behavior—intended to gain benefits that the actor perceives that he or she cannot gain in another way. Most students of organizations consider organizational politics to be relationships taking place outside the legitimate order of the organization (cf., Clegg, at al., 2006). A *political behavior*, then, is an attempt by an organizational actor to maximize gains or to minimize losses by illegitimate means. Note that not all conduct of a political nature is universally immoral or illegal, since it is culturally bound and is subject to change over time.

The following example should clarify this argument. So-called *sexual harassment* in organizations represents one kind of political behavior, since it serves as a means to express the dominance of senior members (e.g., executives) over junior ones (e.g., secretaries). "The sense of power felt by senior employees tacitly implies the temptation to demand from others their submission to bodily contacts of one kind or another against their will" (Samuel, 2005:131). Sexual harassment is, by definition, a clear case of political behavior in organizations. This is self-serving, power-based conduct, which exceeds the limits of legitimate authority.

Nonetheless, until fairly recently gestures such caressing, touching of another person's private parts, flirting, and attempts at sexual coercion were deemed forgivable kinds of misbehavior. In such a social-cultural climate, neither women nor men dared to complain about being victims of sexual harassment by their superiors at the workplace. Even worse, those who did complain encountered a negative reaction on the part of the authorities. Only lately, have the social norms with regard to such conduct dramatically changed in Western countries; sexual harassment is now illegal as well as being socially deviant, carrying severe penalties in law, and eliciting aversion in the public at large.

Another example of organizational politics, which receives different interpretations and encounters different reactions, is bribery. It is common knowledge that today bribery in its various forms still remains a means of exchange in economic transactions in many countries. In those places the practice of giving and taking bribes for the purpose of getting better deals or gaining higher benefits reflects corrupt behavior. This behavior is political in nature, to which the authorities and the public alike turn a blind eye under the pretext, "this is the only way to get things done around here." Bribery is clearly immoral and illegal, therefore, it is condemned outright in First World countries; yet, the same conduct is merely a part of the political reality, therefore, a permissible custom in Third World countries.

Politics in organizations, as discussed so far, has two sides: "objective," as determined by certain parameters (e.g., self-serving, power-based, non-sanctioned) and "subjective." The latter aspect of organizational politics will be identified here by the term *perceived politics* (cf., Vigoda-Gadot and Drory, 2006).

> Organizational politics has another side—the subjective side, which represents the way that members of a given organization perceive some specific intentions and actions of their supervisors, their colleagues or their subordinates as political modes of behavior. Since it concerns actions and interactions that do not correspond to the established rules of behavior, organizational politics reflects, at least from this viewpoint, an irregular phenomenon, one which deviates from the social norms of organizations, as they are expressed in formal rules and procedures. Therefore, for many people, the idea of politics in organizations is perceived as nothing but a manifestation of deviant, harmful, and divisive behavior. (Samuel, 2005:88)

In light of this view of organizational politics, it is not surprising that at least for some scholars, as well as practitioners, organizational politics presents a serious problem that may endanger organizations' wellbeing and ultimately may threaten their long-term survival. About twenty-five years ago, Mintzberg (1983) expressed this point of view with regard to the phenomenon of politics in organizations.

> Politics refers to individual or group behavior that is informal, ostensibly parochial, typically divisive, and above all, in the technical sense, illegitimate—sanctioned neither by formal authority, accepted ideology, nor certified expertise (though it may exploit any one of them. (Mintzberg, 1983:172)

Adopting this negative attitude, many members of organizations, primarily managers and executives, deny the existence of politics in their workplace; at the same time, they dismiss its potential hazards to the wellbeing of their organization. However, organizational politics does have negative implications for members' perceptions of and feelings toward the organization and its top management; it adversely affects their attitude to the workplace and undermines their identification with and commitment to it (Albrecht, 2006). Such reactions indicate the strong influence of perceived politics to the morale of an organization's participants. Moreover, people who resent the idea of politics in the organization to which they belong are more likely to exit and find themselves a less politicized workplace. Such turnover often may result in harmful loss of talent (brain drain), as well as the flight of the most honest members.

Politics may spread all over the organization, dragging more and more participants into political games. Under certain conditions, organizational politics is likely to create a wide range of problems, to the extent that it becomes a real organizational pathology. Like physical disease and mental disorder in human beings, this kind of pathology obstructs the organization's proper functioning, and even endangers its chances of survival.

Intra-Organizational Politics

Inter-Level Politics

Functional conflicts between supervisors and their subordinates encourage resolving such disputes by political means, in ways that exceed the limits of supervisors' authority. For instance, they tend to enforce their will on their subordinates, use their seniority to disseminate disinformation, manipulate their subordinates into doing things they otherwise would not do, impose penalties on those who do not comply with their demands, and isolate non-conforming subordinates from the rest of their workgroups. Supervisors, managers, and executives play this kind of political game to maintain their authority over their subordinates, despite resistance (Mintzberg, 1983).

Still, subordinates who see themselves as victims of their superiors' caprice tend to use political tactics against them. They take their revenge by means of disobedience, expressions of disloyalty, spreading rumors and gossip, and attempting to defame and denounce them (Samuel, 2005). Political games of this kind seek to undermine the authority of managers in the organization (Mintzberg, 1983).

These and similar clashes create turmoil and unrest among members of the organization, compelling them to take sides. The stronger and more extensive such conflicts are, the graver the dire consequences for the entire organization and the danger of its collapse.

Challenging the authority system repeatedly and vigorously exercising power against such challenges poses a real danger to the organization. Such political games—the *insurgency game* and the *counter-insurgency game*—tend to spread throughout the organization and to contaminate its entire body. Eventually that organization will sink below par, down to a state of impasse.

Let us briefly present the following example. During the years 2004 and 2005, Reserve General Ariel Sharon, a former Prime Minister of Israel, planned to evacuate the Israeli settlements from the Gaza Strip and give the territory back to the Palestinians. The decision encountered strong opposition from some members of his own right-wing political party (the Likud). Eventually, Sharon obtained approval for his evacuation plan from his party, the government, and the Parliament (the Knesset). Nevertheless, a group of the Likud Knesset members persistently opposed each of Sharon's initiatives. They attempted to challenge his authority, undermine his leadership, and even force him to step down from the office of prime minister.

The dissidents used manipulations aimed at defeating Sharon's proposed resolutions in the forum known as the Likud Center, a party body of three thousand delegates. The media interpreted their minor victories as humiliation of the leader of the ruling party and a weakening of his power. Sharon took revenge on the so-called "rebels" in the Likud parliamentary faction by denying them senior government posts and ensuring that most of them would remain backbenchers in the Knesset. He ignored them and showed his contempt for them publicly on many occasions. His close circle of aides and advisors ridiculed them and their leader—Benjamin Netanyahu, whose ploy to remove Sharon from power, had failed.

These political games of insurgency and counter-insurgency dragged on, to the point where Sharon, weary with the situation, resigned from the Likud, thereby splitting Israel's largest political party at the time. He and his supporters established a new political party named Kadima ("forward").

In the general elections that soon followed these events the new Kadima party won twice as many votes as the former ruling Likud party had in the previous elections. Ariel Sharon was returned as Prime Minister of Israel for the third time, supported by a large coalition of several parties in the

Knesset. The decimated Likud party forfeited most of its power, losing over one million supporters, and shrinking to become only the fourth largest party in Israel with a Knesset faction of just twelve seats.

This case demonstrates that inter-level politics inside an organization shakes its foundations, splits its members into rival coalitions, and eventually causes dismemberment of the organization altogether. Through episodes of this kind, organizations, public or private, are likely to meet their end. Ongoing power struggles of this sort tend to escalate and become pathological, a condition that needs proper treatment before it gets out of control.

Inter-Group Politics

> All organizations are networks of interest groups, whether professional groupings, work groups, or other divisions. In turn, organizational politics involve the efforts of interest groups to influence decisions that affect their positions in the organization. In each political struggle, interest groups must decide whether to pursue their political goals in isolation from other interest groups or to form a coalition of interest groups in their pursuit of a common goal. (Bacharach and Lawler, 1980:79)

The players in inter-group politics wield a variety of weapons in their power struggles in the organizational arena. They include manipulation, pressure, threats, negotiations, coalition formation, and lobbying, as well as acts of violence.

The concept of *social group* in this context refers to work groups whose members maintain close interpersonal ties on a daily basis (e.g., working teams)—formal departments and divisions, consisting of many participants; trade unions and professional associations; demographic categories of people such as females, dark-skinned people, labor migrants, and the like. Since these entire groups feel deprived, they join in the *political game* that proceeds on both the inside and outside the organizational levels to improve their working conditions.

As long as inter-group politics follows conventional tracks (negotiation and bargaining) not much harm befalls the organization. But when it escalates to a 'political war' between such groups the entire organization gets into real trouble. The use of more aggressive and violent means by one group against the other creates an *intense conflict*. They tend to spill over and to pervade the entire organization. Then the contestants become more interested in winning the game, per se, than in attaining their initial goals. People are likely to respond emotionally to the others' challenges, to attack their foes in ways meant to hurt them, and to retaliate with even stronger measures than those of their opponents.

Escalation processes of this kind exist in the realm of organizations everywhere. For instance, labor disputes often lead to the use of sanctions, strikes, acts of sabotage, financial penalties, work stoppages, closure of sites, and even injuries to people on either side. The real danger of such measures lies in their likelihood of recurrence repeatedly. At work organizations where such conflicts prevail, labor relations turn into pathological conditions that grow worse with time. First, the level of hostility between the two parties rises from one clash to the next. The conflicting parties then talk less and fight more. Consequently, clients, suppliers, investors, and others suffer increasing damages; such organizations have to cope with a bad reputation in the eyes of their clients. Finally, organizations that are unable to resolve such conflicts deteriorate to the point of no return and they are doomed to die.

Politicization of an organization clearly generates enormous stress on its members; it leads to repeated clashes among interest groups; and it piles up direct and indirect costs. Extensive politics is therefore counter-productive, since it is likely to engender more problems than it is capable of solving.

> Few organizations can sustain a state of intense conflict. In other words, the complete Political Arena cannot last: It represents a valid tendency but an unlikely stable state. The complete Political Arena simply demands too much energy for what it offers in return. Eventually it must consume all of the organization's resources, and kill it. (Mintzberg, 1983:430)

Let us follow now the example of detrimental competition presented earlier (see Chapter 3). Following a structural change made in that high-tech enterprise in the defense industry, its four main production-line divisions started to function as profit centers, redefined as *strategic business units* (SBU) of that organization. Each division had its unique expertise and its own line of goods, but all of them were interdependent with regard to the design, development, and production of special components needed for their products.

As already stated, the restructuring compelled the separate divisions to compete for government bids on large-scale projects, both inside the country and abroad. In short time, the divisions found themselves competing with each other against external organizations. Their drive to win such projects as chief contractors and their lack of experience in the realm of business induced them to cut their prices considerably.

Bound by the commitments made by its divisions, the focal organization was compelled to supply goods at non-profitable prices. The division heads and their subordinates started to accuse one another of irresponsible behavior, refrained from cooperation, and tried to pull the rug out from under the feet of their partners in the organization. Political conduct of this kind created tension, antagonism, and a stressful environment. The CEO complained, "My division heads are cutting each other's throat." The organization was losing its main advantage: the synergy among its varieties of core competencies. Moreover, it was losing money at the expense of the taxpayer. Not surprisingly, influential figures such as private sector executives and politicians cast doubt on the idea of turning a state-owned agency into a business enterprise at all.

In sum, the focal organization displayed a series of symptoms that resemble a serious illness in organisms. Since then, and despite its grave situation, the organization managed to turn around—slowly but steadily, due to its partial privatization.

Still, as could be expected, this *detrimental competition* between subunits proved dysfunctional to the organization as a whole. The pathological nature of such political games has been manifested time and again until today. Recently, in an attempt to halt the perils of such politics, the top management induced another major structural change, in which it dismantled a major division and reframed the territories of the remaining divisions.

Inter-Organizational Politics

Senior executives are usually the actors who initiate and decide to take part in certain "political games" between their organization and others. Such politics allegedly aims to improve the bargaining position of the organizations involved over their rivals. Inter-organizational politics serve the individuals who take part in these games to increase their own benefits as well. Politics at this level seems to be a rather tricky business, since it may easily spill over to illegal activities such as corporate crime.

Political maneuvers of organizations against others cannot be hidden for long from the public's ears and eyes. The media, law enforcement agencies, the stock market, as well as competitors and rivals are very likely to disseminate information of this kind. Even in cases where politics does not transgress the legal borders it is still self-serving behavior intended to take unfair advantage of other organizations by the exercise of power against them, whether overtly or covertly.

The targets of such politics are often problematic organizations at a stage of decline, crisis, disorder, or failure, which a priori are weaker than their rivals. Organizations that have to cope with severe internal problems can barely withstand power struggles and political games against strong external forces. Their rivals are likely to take them up whole or break them into pieces. Inter-organizational politics, then, is liable to wipe out organizations that are in deep trouble.

Politics among organizations assumes a variety of forms in everyday life; some of them are subtle, others rather stinging. In this chapter we shall focus on three common forms of inter-organizational politics, namely, *competition, partnership,* and *dominance.* "Each of these forms is based on the power of the organizations involved in these relationships, and it reflects the way in which the organizations actually exercise their power against their rivals" (Samuel, 2005:174).

Competition Politics

Business firms compete with other organizations for potential clients, investors, suppliers, contractors, specialists, and so forth. As long as competition is conducted fairly, and the rivals employ conventional strategies (e.g., reaching out to new markets) and tactics (e.g., advertisements), it is seemingly a legitimate commercial contest. However, the exercise of power over competitors (e.g., coercion, manipulation) diverts the commercial competition to the arena of inter-organizational politics. There it is liable to escalate to the point where the parties involved attempt to crush their rivals and cause them real damage.

Under certain circumstances, organizations do not hesitate to use "dirty" political tactics (e.g., espionage, disinformation, intimidation) to advance their interests. To survive, the targets of such manipulations are compelled to defend themselves. They frequently do so by the use of their own political counter-measures. Acts of denunciation, defamation, casting suspicion, and accusations are just a few forms of reprisal. The competition turns into a battle in which illegitimate means serve to attain legitimate goals.

Here is one example of a political fray. A well-established corporation in the telecommunications industry was losing clients who were replacing their landline telephones with cellular ones. Other novel means of communication (e.g., electronic mail, calling cards) added their share to the continuing decrease of regular telephone services. Soon the same telephone company encountered another kind of competition, this time from cable TV enterprises, which started to sell cheap telephone services through their cable infrastructure.

According to press reports, the telephone company discreetly approached employees of their competitors offering them various gifts, vouchers, free services, and other privileges (but not cash) in return for lists of their employer's new clients. These lists are classified "trump cards," which any commercial organization keeps close to its chest. This kind of espionage is by any standard an illegitimate mode of competition and since it allegedly involves bribery, it may even be brought to the court of law.

The target organization sought out its employees who had committed a breach of trust by furnishing such sensitive information to the competitor. It publicly accused the other organization of playing dirty; it fired its guilty employees; and it prepared a lawsuit against the owners of the competitor.

Given the economic strength of the infiltrated organization, this situation is not likely to be fatal. Still, some damages, such as feeling of mistrust between members, may prove harmful in the near future; mutual accusations of disloyalty are likely to exacerbate stressful situations and lower employee morale. The management is likely to tighten monitoring and control of employees' conduct, and the number of whistleblowers will probably grow.

The alleged spying organization may encounter serious difficulties because of its attempt to bribe a competitor's employees. Should a court find this organization guilty, it may experience grave problems in terms of income and reputation. Some employees, mainly managers who disapprove of such unethical behavior by their employer, are likely to quit this workplace. In light of such allegations, clients and investors may reconsider their existing or potential business dealings with a provider of communication services that can no longer be trusted. These and other negative responses inside and outside the organization may cause illegitimate political gambits like this to boomerang, which eventually prove fatal.

Partnership Politics

More and more organizations of various kinds prefer to cooperate rather than compete with their rivals. Under certain conditions, cooperation is likely to yield greater benefits than competition would do. Nowadays, numerous organizational networks, joint ventures, multi-organizational consortia, inter-organizational coalitions, and interlocking directories form various kinds of partnerships. These improve the partners' bargaining position, give them an edge over others, and provide them with exclusive information. All these factors are advantageous from a political viewpoint.

Yet, achieving this generally beneficial inter-organizational cooperation requires the use of political means, which are not necessarily legitimate and sometimes are even illegal. Organizational networks may turn into business cartels, which many countries forbid by the law; organizational partners may exchange inside information secretly for the purpose of buying or selling shares in the stock market; they could set up hidden coalitions to yield them much greater power in their clashes with labor unions. Inter-organizational partnerships often serve as means for the attainment of dominance in various markets.

Alongside their advantages, the various kinds of partnerships have built-in disadvantages. Often the partners do not entirely trust each other. In the first place, many joint ventures, consortia, and networks consist of members that are otherwise competitors. In fact, they persist in their competition despite being partners, jeopardizing the partnership's chances of survival (Parker and Russo, 1996). They conclude restraining contracts and agreements, but they can hardly conform to them as partners. Inter-organizational partnerships are liable to be awash with political games, through which the partners try to maximize their benefits at the expense of their counter-parts. The more prevalent such political games and power struggles, the greater their peril to the wellbeing and survival of the partnerships.

Like single organizations, partnerships too may have to endure various types of pathologies such as distrust, disobedience, disinformation, deceit, and betrayal. This kind of malignant state of affairs between partners and between their representatives may prove responsible for the disintegration of networks, joint ventures, alliances, consortia, and the like.

Takeover Politics

Needless to say, organizations—business as well as other kinds—have to cope continually with a variety of threats endangering their wellbeing and even their survival. To safeguard the supply lines of critical resources (e.g., raw materials, capital, workforce) many of them, mainly the bigger and stronger ones, attempt to perform so-called *vertical integration*. Numerous organizations try to eliminate their competitors and other rivals by *horizontal integration*. One way or another, both strategies reflect takeover of one organization or more. "Frequently, this takeover is carried out against the will of the organization's ownership and its governance, and is therefore identified as *hostile takeover*" (Samuel, 2005:186).

Organizations take others over by means of manipulation, intimidation, or coercion. This kind of inter-organizational politics is likely to prove deadly to the organizations taken over by such hostile means, which are often eradicated as independent, viable entities. Actually, the so-called *inter-organizational mergers* may not differ from takeovers since they serve as disguised means by some partners to swallow their counter-parts. Not surprisingly, a considerable proportion of mergers eventually fail. Such failures are far more often the result of social and cultural differences between the merged organizations than of financial difficulties faced by the new entity.

Employees are likely to perceive mergers as acts of acquisition or takeover of their workplace, mainly when a giant multinational corporate merges with a fairly small local enterprise. In such cases, mergers evoke feelings of resentment among employees of both parties; they stimulate attitudes of alienation from the other partner; and members lack any sense of identification with the new organizational assemblage. These and similar feelings are likely to be enhanced mainly in mergers where employees are transferred from one site to another, where new managers replace the former ones, and where new rules of conduct are imposed. Many employees cannot or do not want to adapt to the new working conditions because for them mergers merely represent political games played by powerful stakeholders, who tend to disregard the interests of the powerless workers. These negative reactions then emerge in abnormal patterns of behavior such as aggression, estrangement, or quitting.

Conclusion

There is no argument nowadays that the phenomenon of organizational politics is ubiquitous. This notion refers to various attempts by organizational actors to increase their benefits beyond what they are entitled to. Politics in this context refers to sets of activities that are essentially power-based, self-serving, and non-sanctioned. In this sense, politics represents the darker side of organizations. This is where individuals, groups, and organizations gain or lose extra benefits due to various kinds of manipulation, wrangling, and compromise.

Political games take place on at least three levels of activities: among individual participants (*micro politics*), among intra-organizational groups (*meso politics*) and subunits, and among different organizations of various kinds (*macro politics*). On the micro-level, subordinates and supervisors are frequently engaged in conflicts in which the former struggle to undermine their superiors' authority, whereas the latter enforce their will on the rebels. Each party wields its own power against the other. When such inter-level struggles constantly recur, they generate a great deal of stress inside the organization, they compel participants to take sides, and they evoke reciprocal feelings of resentment and hostility. At a certain point an organizational pathology is likely to evolve. Consequently, the normal conduct of the organization is susceptible to serious impairment.

Political struggles between social groups that are based on demographic differences (e.g., gender, ethnicity) are most likely to take place in various kinds of organizations nowadays. Such intergroup conflicts are divisive in nature, nurturing feelings of relative deprivation, and complaints of injustice. Those who get fewer benefits demand a greater share of the spoils, at the expense of those who get more, whereas the latter fight to preserve their privileges. Continuous friction of this kind contributes to neither the health nor the wealth of an organization.

Internal competition between subunits (e.g., divisions) reflects another kind of conflict on the meso-level. Such rivalries are counter-productive as they sub-optimize the gains of some units at the expense of the organization's profits as a whole. They constitute a detrimental strategy, which eventually does more harm than good to the organization at large.

On the macro-level, organizations conduct political games of various kinds aimed at gaining the edge over their competitors. Broadly, they may be classified into three political strategies: competition, partnership, and takeover. They reflect political courses of action based on the exercise of power and the use of illegitimate means. Industrial espionage, falsehood, and defamation are just a few means of fraudulent competition. Hidden cartels, exchange of classified information, and setting up of unlawful networks demonstrate how organization gains the advantage through fake partnerships. Mergers and acquisitions are often merely takeovers, perpetrated to throw competitors out of the market or to dominate suppliers of critical resources.

In sum, the implications of organizational politics are by no means negligible. Politics may prove harmful to organizations, as it is liable to nurture various pathologies. As discussed in this chapter, under certain conditions organizational politics may threaten the survival of organizations and, indeed, kill them.

7

Greed and Corruption

Corruption, it seems, is everywhere, afflicting for-profit, not-for-profit, governmental, and to the dismay of many, even religious organizations. Further, corrupt behavior seems to be strongly associated not only with individuals within organizations but also with organizations themselves. (Blake, et al., 2008:670)

Probably one of the most harmful causes of failing organizations is so-called *White-Collar Crime* of their senior officers. According to one definition, white-collar crime is "an illegal act or series of illegal acts committed by nonphysical means and by concealment or guile, to obtain money or property, to avoid payment or loss of money or property, or to obtain business or personal advantage" (Edelhertz, 1970:19-20).

Some executives, accountants, directors, and other high-ranking officers abuse their power of office to gain extra, unwarranted benefits by illegitimate means, such as deceit, forgery, theft, or bribery. Probably more rank-and-file employees engage in criminal acts as such. Either way, according to Agency Theory, the prime beneficiary of such activities is the agent, that is, the corrupt individual (Pinto, et al., 2008:687).

Considering the significant rates of lawbreaking by members of the general public in many countries (Gabor, 1994), it should not be surprising to realize that employees are likely to commit a variety of offenses in their workplace. However, in most cases the damage to the organization caused by high-ranking officers is far greater than that of low-ranking ones.

Senior officers are able to steal enormous sums of their organization's money by sophisticated methods, they can also harvest excessive profits by manipulation of stocks and/or commodities in their respective markets, and they can report fictitious transactions and hide payments deep in their own pockets. Aside from the legal aspects of such fraud, it causes moral damage to the organization, which jeopardizes its reputation and credibility vis-à-vis its clientele and the public at large. Since leaders' corruption in certain organizations is usually not merely a single act of succumbing to temptation but a pattern, it evolves as a pathology that eventually afflicts the entire organization and threatens its survival. The collapse of Enron serves as an infamous example of this phenomenon (e.g., Bryce, 2003; Cruver, 2002). However, as Levine (2005:724) argues, corruption in organizations is rather more complicated than merely the unlawful conduct of some members.

> Criminal conduct, however, does not in itself sustain the charge of corruption. For corruption, there must be something more than mere criminal conduct, something more than the effort to get rich at the end. For corruption there must be perversion of a higher end especially a public trust. This means that, for crime to rise to the level of corruption, we must also find a disconnection from significant norms. My concern is with the way individuals do or do not become securely attached to norms; and with how individuals who fail to develop such attachments develop in their place certain of the qualities associated with corruption: greed, arrogance, a sense of personal entitlement, the idea of virtue as personal loyalty, and the inability to distinguish between organizational and personal ends.

Briefly, the concept of corruption refers to "improper and usually unlawful conduct intended to secure a benefit for oneself or another. Its forms include bribery, extortion, and misuse of inside information" (Encyclopaedia Britannica Online, 2009).

Yet, corruption is not merely inefficiency caused by bad management or by incompetent performers. The notion of corruption in this context implies deliberate intent of individuals to maximize their personal gains illegally at the expense of the organization. In this sense, corruption is typically an egoistic conduct driven by an individual's preference of self over anybody else. In other words, the primary beneficiary of corrupt behavior is the individual himself (Pinto et al., 2008). On the other hand, as it is discussed in detail in the next chapter, some forms of corruption are driven by the will to help ones' organization and to strengthen its standing vis à vis the public by the application of illegitimate means. That is by means of "corporate crime."

Under some circumstances, however, such fraudulent behavior is imposed on oneself by external pressures, threats, or blackmail. Whatever the reasons are, corruption in organizations is like a malignant disease in organisms. It starts somewhere, most likely at the top, and then it spreads down throughout the organizational body. Once junior employees realize that the senior managers are corrupt, they also want some part of the spoil for themselves. Thus, greed takes the place of loyalty; members loot the organizational wealth for their selfish goals. This is a pathology that may drag the organization down and eventually even bring about its final destruction.

The Greed Motive

Among the various motives for individuals' corruption, *greed* is probably the most prevalent. Although the desire to gain more income is ubiquitous in human society, the notion of greed applies to individuals pursuing the fulfillment of such a desire at the expense of others' ability to satisfy their needs and to prevent others' gaining access to those material resources. So, greed denotes a selfish behavior, which most often crosses normative lines—moral, cultural, ethical, or legal. The pressing desire in such people to get rich quickly, no matter what, drives them to ignore the likelihood of being caught, downplaying the negative consequences.

Research evidence indicates time and again that money is a very important factor in the meaning of work among employees around the world (e.g., Mitchell and Mickel, 1999; Du and Tang, 2005). That is because money serves as an indicator of success, as a symbol of status, and vehicle for upward mobility. But people learn to desire money as a goal in itself, rather than just as a means for attaining other goals.

Furthermore, people learn to desire money as a goal, not just as a means for attaining other goals. Hence, greed becomes widespread in many countries. In the Judeo-Christian tradition, greed is seen as the root of all evil. Nevertheless, certain economic, social, and cultural forces in Western societies motivate people to love money and to pursue greater income, hence, to be greedy. Thus, greed encourages corruption in organizations in both the public and the private sectors.

In the former sector, Rivlin (2003:348) maintains, "the stakes are not primarily financial rewards. They are votes, public approval, and retention of power. But some of the temptations are the same—to fudge the numbers, shade the truth, and downplay the potential risks of a course of action." However, corrupt conduct as such usually involves considerable sums of payoff money for concealment. Whatever the purpose of such misconduct, greed is most likely to be an integral part of corruption.

Consider the following example. A large construction company just recently collapsed. This was a private enterprise, owned and managed by one family. For forty years that company built thousands of residential buildings, hotels, central stations, and the like at many construction sites. The company also owned several public international subsidiaries, which did business in several countries. In response to rumors about the company's financial difficulties, hundreds of clients broke into their unfinished apartments in order to establish their claims of ownership. As the company collapsed, the CEO escaped the country to an unknown destination, carrying large bundle of cash money with him. He left behind him a debt of over $400 million, 4500 families without a roof over their heads, and 1200 families who may lose their investments altogether. Police investigations revealed that the CEO and his accomplices had allegedly made various illegal transfers of the clients' payments to secrete bank accounts. They lied to many naïve clients about their right to get bank guarantees of their payments should the company fail, giving them instead minor discounts on the cost of their apartments. They had not paid their large debts to their suppliers and subcontractors, as well as committing other fraudulent acts. About one month after the collapse, Interpol discovered the CEO's hideaway abroad. Since then, he was extradited to his country of origin. There, he was indicted of theft, deceit, and fraud and, accordingly sentenced for seven years in prison and heavy fine.

The temptation to acquire extra income by unethical as well as illegal means leads employees of lower ranks to steal company assets belonging to their employers. Employee theft causes a great deal of damage to the employing organizations and to the national economy at large. According to Vardi and Weitz (2004:4-5), "Undoubtedly, OMB [Organizational Misbehavior] comes with a hefty price tag. With the cost comes a growing awareness of it. Estimates of the costs of the most prevalent misbehavior—employee theft—run as high as $200 billion annually in the United States alone" (Greenberg, 1997).

Some scholars provide various explanations for employee thievery such as meager wages, lack of essential fringe benefits, and job insecurity (e.g., Greenberg, 1993). However, theft in the name of justice serves as an excuse for all kinds of corruption in organizations. For instance, in some parts of the world (e.g., Africa and South America) bribery is culturally embedded. Civil servants, law enforcers, drivers, shop stewards, and a various incumbents of other occupations get extra payoffs for their services. It is no wonder then that their clients have to pay them off. However, the custom of bribery as an integral part of any transaction apparently does not stop at the lower ranks of organizations. Senior officials and executives in both the public and private sectors of those countries request, and indeed get, hefty payoffs, mainly for approving trade contracts. Similarly, high-level politicians obtain their share of the spoils to cover their personal living costs and to pay the bills of their extravagant lifestyles.

A former Israeli Minister of Treasury has long been under investigation by the police, suspected of taking a large cut of monies stolen from the labor federation, of which he served as chairman. According to the press, several senior officials regularly withdrew checks for millions of New Israel Shekels from the federation's bank accounts. A trusted messenger transferred some part of the money to the chairman's personal bank account. Brown bags containing bundles of cash money would be delivered directly to his home. For over seven years he received "monthly expenses" for his trips abroad, holiday gifts, medications, meals in fancy restaurants, and entertaining members of his political party. In addition, he requested, and received, cash for his election primaries campaign. Thus, the chairman of a voluntary association, together with his senior officials, was stealing money paid as membership fees and for the association's various services.

This kind of theft exemplifies the power of greed to drive affluent executives to steal money from their organizations so as to maintain a lavish style of living. This kind of theft is not due to a pressing need for survival, nor is it an act by the underprivileged that deem it justified because of their deprivation. Executive misconduct of this kind reflects greed-driven corruption. This example further shows that corruption is not a "one-man show." For a senior employee to abuse his or her ability to access the organization's assets, he or she needs the cooperation of others that are as greedy. The possession of power in organizations does change the mindset of onlookers. They are more likely to take advantage of their positions for their own benefit at the expense of others, including their organization. They tend to impose their will on subordinates, by the promise of reward or the threat of penalties. Hence, their motivation and their ability pave the way to corrupt behavior of various kinds. Not surprisingly, power does corrupt, as the hoary proverb says. The so-called *white-collar crime* differs from ordinary theft because the former is legally considered a *betrayal of trust*—a much more serious offense than mere theft. In contrast, some scholars apply this concept to a much wider variety of offences than those related to the breach of trust (e.g., Edelhertz, 1983; Ashforth et al., 2008)).

Numerous cases of fraudulent behavior by senior managers in the private sector are easily found, but many more can probably be found in the public sector in every country. For example, the media just disclosed that top-level politicians in the United Kingdom got reimbursement for their rather odd, private expenses.

Among the culprits are police officers, customs inspectors, and intelligence agents, not to mention judges, warders, and immigration officials.

The media report such cases daily everywhere. Although the corrupt ones are a minority, in the public eye they represent a corruption culture.

Overall, greed-driven corruption is rather pathological, first, because it tempts others to dip their hands into the till as well. Second, it creates an atmosphere of distrust among clients, suppliers, and partners in the organization. Third, it imperils the loyalty of organization members, mainly of those in the lower ranks. Finally, greed-driven corruption shakes the moral foundation of the organization, namely, the premises and values to which people adhere in that context.

In light of these consequences, corrupt executives in the private sector jeopardize the survival of the entire organization. Still, government agencies are less likely to die and vanish. Instead, their corrupt officials introduce "a state of sickness," characterized by symptoms of unhealthy organizations. Expressions of employees' alienation and apathy, low morale, poor reputation, suspicions, accusations, and rumor spreading represent a few symptoms of such situations. To help the organization to recover, some cures are likely to be introduced, such as rapid replacement of senior officials by outside candidates, extensive discharge of lower ranking members, tightening of control measures, and introduction of new rules and procedures. If those measures do not rescue the focal organization, it is likely to fail.

Political Corruption

"Political corruption occurs when an agent breaks the law in sacrificing the interest of a principal to his or her own benefit" (Heywood, 1997:6). According to della Porta and Vannuci (1999), "corruption refers to the abuse of public resources for private gain, through a hidden transaction that involves the violation of some standards of behavior." Following these definitions, political corruption should be considered a specific pathology rather than a general disease. This is so, due to its detrimental consequences to the organization at large.

However, we have to recognize that so-called *political corruption* is a multifaceted phenomenon in the realm of today's politics. In this chapter, we concentrate only on those manifestations that are most relevant to the context of the present volume.

About a quarter of century ago, the sociologist Amitai Etzioni devoted an entire book to the issue of political corruption in America, using the term *plutocracy*, which refers to the linkage between wealth (Greek *ploutos*) and power (*kratos*).

Plutocracy does *not* assume one ruling class, or one-power elite, as the Marxists would have us believe. America's power wielders include a variety of groups—corporations and labor unions, big business and associations of small businesses, oil companies and farm associations and banks. They do not all pull in the same direction, they are not in cahoots with one another, like one well-organized, tidy bunch. On the contrary, each interest group seeks to tilt the system in its own way, so that the riches on the table will roll into its own pockets. Cumulatively, however, they do prevent the government from discharging its appointed duties, from serving the public first and foremost. (Etzioni, 1984:4)

This form of political corruption refers to the influence of various wealthy groups and organizations on public officials to use their power in ways that support the particular economic interests of the influential. Quite often, this kind of favoritism comes at the expense of the public at large. In most countries the so-called "money elite" consists of tycoons, oligarchs, oil barons, media moguls, real-estate sharks, capitalists, and even mafiosi who maintain close ties with figures among the power elite. Such important stakeholders are likely to take advantage of their wealth and power to bribe politicians, promote governmental officials, to infiltrate their aides into key positions where they can weigh the dice in favor of their patrons.

Above all, the influential make sure that their favorite candidates win the elections by donations of massive illegal funds through hidden financial channels. That money goes towards intense political propaganda in its various forms. It also helps to pay for frequent public opinion surveys and preliminary polls. In addition, this money pays legions of assistants, writers, public relations experts, and political consultants. Needless to say, the money elite expect to benefit later from their investments in the election campaigns; this turns their donations into actual bribery.

It is not surprising that once elections end in any democratic country, politicians tend to accuse their rivals of accepting forbidden donations of an illegal and/or unethical nature. Usually, the first to accuse their political rivals are those who have lost the elections. However, the winners do not hesitate to strike back at the losers with similar accusations, to justify their victory. A considerable share of candidates seem to obtain the private money of wealthy businesspeople, giant corporations, interest groups, and affluent families; these pump in large funds, which exceed the legal limits.

In return for their pre-election support, the elected politicians often "take care" of their patrons. Those legislators reciprocate favors to their supporters in the form of tax exemptions, favorable legislation, budgetary appropriations, subsidies, licenses, contracts, and similar privileges. In light of the enormous wealth of individual donors and the large scale of their corporations, those privileges are by no means negligible. This kind of *quid pro quo* between "business patrons" and "political protégés" is neither explicit nor contractual in any form, but the latter feel obliged to the former, and they are familiar with their partners' interests. Such an implicit exchange corrupts the political system: it constitutes "the use of public office for private advantage" (Etzioni, 1984:4).

In at least some cases the patrons are part of organized crime. "Where organized crime is deep-rooted, corruption finds a particularly fertile soil…The Mafia and the politicians invest different types of resources in these exchanges. And each derives numerous advantages from them" (della Porta and Vannuci, 1999:221). In Italy, for example, *Cosa Nostra* (i.e., organized crime) has used the weapon of violence against politicians who refused to take part in this game most effectively. Hence, mutual protection exists between high-level, corrupt politicians and important Mafia bosses.

> Even in developed countries some legitimate businesses are especially vulnerable to criminal infiltration. Organized crime is both wealthy and unscrupulous. It is willing to use not only bribery but also threats and violence to enforce its contracts and get its way. In the most successful examples the legitimate businesses which operate under Mafia protection earn sufficient monopoly rents to make them supporters of continued organized-crime influence. (Rose-Ackerman, 1999:23)

Another form of political corruption is *nepotism*. In democratic countries, where the civil service should render uniform service to the public at large, should be politically pure, and should adhere to ethical norms and obey the law, nepotism and similar forms of favoritism are symptoms of corruption.

"*Nepotistic* corruption refers to the unjustified appointment of friends or relatives to public office, or according them favored treatment" (Heywood, 1997:10). Nepotism goes into effect whenever government agencies adhere to a custom of hiring their employees' relatives, preferring them to other qualified job applicants. A high rate of relatives' employment creates a built-in problem in the organization. Systematic appointment of relatives in one public organization may create relations of subordination between family members; it enhances conflicts of interest among them; and it brings together large groups of family members, which is likely to worsen the efficiency of that organization. Preference of relatives in the workplace may also prevent equal employment opportunity of non-relatives; and it leads to under-representation of social groups that do not happen to have relatives among the employees of that organization. This state of affairs may harm public trust in governmental agencies and their quality of services. Above all, nepotism is a breach of civil servants' loyalty to the taxpayers and to the public at large.

Table 7.1 illustrates this improper tendency in the public service. The table presents the findings of an inspection conducted by Israel's State Comptroller of a sample of state-owned corporations. The findings clearly indicate symptoms of political corruption, as they show high rates of relatives, as much as 44% of the total employees. Such a systematic preference for relatives does not conform to the norm of competence in the public service. Even worse, most of these employees enjoy the safety of tenure, and they are members of strong labor unions.

Therefore, it is very difficult to discharge them regardless of how they entered these organizations. Given that these corporations render vital services, they are not likely to cease in spite of their corruption. However, they are subject to privatization, whenever the government decides to remove them from the public sector. In that case, they are likely to undergo profound changes intended to "cleanse them" of corrupt favoritism.

Another well-known form of political corruption is the *spoils system*. This is "a practice in which the political party winning an election re-

Table 7.1
Employment of Workers in Eight Public Corporations*

Name of Corporation	Total Number of Employees	Number of Relatives	Rate of Employed Relatives (percent)
Airports Authority	3,121	692	22%
Israel Railway Company	1,730	220	13%
Ashdod Seaport Company	1,176	519	44%
Haifa Seaport Company	988	248	25%
Israel Postal Company	4,966	724	15%
Israel Electricity Company	13,222	3,551	27%
National Water Company	2,100	288	14%
Petroleum Infrastructures & Energy Company	381	23	6%
Total	27,684	6,265	23%

Source: Israel State Comptroller's *Annual Report*, 2007, vol. 58A. p. 13.

*In some of the inspected corporations more distant relatives were also employed, but since they are not legally defined as relatives they are not included in this table.

wards its campaign workers and other active supporters by appointment to government posts and by other favours. The spoils system involves political activity by public employees in support of their party and the employees' removal from office if their party loses the election" (Encyclopedia Britannica Online, 2009).

Apparently, this improper conduct has developed deep roots in the soil of the civil service of various democratic countries. It starts with the misconduct of high-ranking officers, such as ministers and general managers, and it spreads all the way down to lower ranks. The beneficiaries of this corrupt system of appointments would barely qualify for their jobs but for their proximity to the senior politicians in power.

For example, a few years ago a former government minister was charged with systematically appointing members of his political party to various offices, some of them fictitious, in his department. An investigation of the state comptroller revealed the appointment of political supporters to a large number of jobs, which meant riding roughshod over the law and the rules of sound administration. Such misconduct by a senior member of the government constituted politicization of the public sector and abuse of public resources for the advancement of his personal interests. The minister denied his guilt, arguing that the so-called corrupt system of appointments was simply a common norm adopted by other politicians as well. Such a phenomenon indicates the corrupt behavior of senior politicians in a democratic country. Presumably, a similar pattern of appointments is likely to be found in local government too.

Once the spoils system penetrates the public sector, successful political candidates campaigning for their election are obliged to pay for their victory by handing out jobs to their aides and supporters. The pressures exerted on these officials to conduct such an exchange distorts the principle of merit in the public service; they cast a deep shadow upon the integrity of public representatives (e.g., ministers, members of the parliament, mayors, and commissioners); and they transform at least some parts of the public administration into corrupt systems of civil service.

The spread of political corruption becomes a sort of malignancy that can be extirpated from the civil service only with difficulty. As anyone can see, in a considerable number of countries worldwide today the public sector is contaminated with various kinds of political corruption. In those places, various modes of illegal exchange are part of the culture and perceived as common norms, albeit informally. Individuals and organizations alike learn to join in the political game of give-and-take to their advantage.

In established democracies, however, this kind of conduct by politicians is in every sense criminal. Accordingly, corrupt politicians and officials may be vulnerable targets to all kinds of hidden pressures, threats, and blackmail. To protect both their power and their reputation they may have no other choice but to surrender to their pursuers by rewarding them, as illegitimate as their demands may be. Thus, "one sin leads to another."

In sum, political corruption entails some negative consequences. First, corruption leads to a distorted supply of the public demand for important goods and services. Second, it causes significant elevation of governmental costs of public projects, since contractors include the cost of bribery in their proposals. Third, corrupt officials abuse their authority by putting in the "fast lane" or putting in the "slow lane" various matters (e.g., proposals, appeals, bids) for hidden reasons. Fourth, corruption leads to "adverse" selection of firms as producers and suppliers of goods and services—firms that otherwise would not qualify for the given role. Fifth, political corruption creates erosion of confidence in the state as an impartial representative of public interests. Lastly, corruption undermines the legitimacy of the government and the political system of the country (della Porta and Vannuci, 1997).

"Ideological" Corruption

Plenty of organizations all over the world—public as well as private—experience episodes of misconduct by some of their members based on their convictions. Those individuals commit such offenses on behalf of a specific cause, not necessarily an honorable one. They disclose classified material, use sabotage, trigger agitation, spread rumor of defamation, and encourage revolt and defection.

Here we call this kind of misconduct, based on specific beliefs rather than greed, "*ideological*" *corruption*; it is perpetrated in particular organizations. Corrupt members of this kind break the law, damage the organization, or betray their co-workers in the name of seemingly religious beliefs, social viewpoints, patriotic feelings, or other personal philosophies. They are willing to commit acts of violence making themselves vulnerable to serious personal risk, irrespective of the material costs and benefits. They deliberately attempt to harm the organizations to which they belong as members, employees, or citizens.

Like other kinds of corruption, "ideological corruption" may be deeply rooted in certain organizations as some of its ideas diffuse through their internal social networks. The more individuals adopt such ideas, the higher the likelihood of their implementation despite the dangers. For example, the former Communist parties in Europe used to "plant" small hidden cells of their members inside numerous workplaces, preparing them to rebel when the time was ripe. Conscientious objectors who are compelled to perform military service tend to persuade their comrades to refrain from tasks that they identify as the immoral exercise of force. They assume that the greater the number of conscripts who refuse to perform such tasks, the lesser the likelihood of facing a court martial. However, in quite a few cases such resistance has entailed loss of life, defeat in battle, or retreat from a holding line in the battlefield.

Some religious sects persuade people to steal money and property from their employing organizations to help the sect's purposes. Other ideological groups pursuing specific agendas may put pressures on their proponents to disclose inside information, to smuggle out classified documents, and to slander colleagues—all for the sake of their cause. For instance, during the Cold War, several high-ranking officials and top politicians in the United Kingdom secretly committed such acts of treason in favor of the Soviet Union.

As may be expected, some "conscientious" men and women commit illegal acts as part of their fight against corruption in their organizations. Among them are naïve whistleblowers who disclose to the press alleged acts of corruption by high-ranking officials. Other individuals disseminate rumors of improper practices taking place in their own organization. In other cases, such individuals reveal misbehavior of public organizations. They do so by publishing "investigative" articles or books, using classified material to substantiate their accusations. The majority of such publications focus on security agencies, police forces, military units, and defense industries of various countries. By this form of defamation, these writers undermine the reputation of the civil service and the integrity of its officials; at the same time, they often break codes of ethics as well as a number of laws.

As people have much more sympathy for misconduct driven by values and beliefs, whatever they are, than for greed-driven misconduct, perpetrators of the former are more likely to be excused for their improper acts than perpetrators of the latter. But the damage to the organization is the same in both cases. From the present viewpoint, whatever the motives may be, corruption in organizations is like a disease that evolves into a built-in pathology. It puts at risk the strength, legitimacy, and life chances of those organizations.

Professional Corruption

The term *professional corruption* refers to unethical or improper professional conduct by doctors, lawyers, engineers, and similar specialists who are employed as practitioners in the public sector (e.g., hospitals, courts of law). It refers to deliberate malpractice, serving professionals to increase their utility such as higher income, higher status, or greater power and influence. Criminologists refer to such offenses as *white-collar corruptions* (Sutherland, 1949; Edelhertz, 1970; Clinard and Yeager, 2006).

Professional corruption is driven by greed and the quest of power or prestige. The public healthcare industry is probably the most prone to various kinds of professional corruption on account of the enormous amounts of money involved in it, the large number of professionals employed there, and the giant pharmaceutical corporations that consistently pour more and more medications into this huge market. So, public healthcare may serve here as an example of corruption that may be found in other public services as well. Once again, we should bear in mind that our interest in this kind of corruption is in its pathological nature and its consequences for such organizations.

Naturally, the medical services of renowned specialists (e.g., heart surgeons, oncologists, gynecologists) are in great demand. Since they cannot treat so many patients, and the lines waiting for operations and treatments are rather long, some of them abuse their reputation and give preference to patients who pay them "under the table" and in advance. These specialists are full-time employees of public hospitals, so they actually use the public facilities of their institution (e.g., operating rooms, equipment, medical supplies) for preferential treatment of their patients. Moreover, such patients are likely to be assigned surgery very quickly, whereas others must wait their turn for lengthy periods of time. Affluent patients can afford the regular, expensive fees of the best private practitioners for treatment at home or abroad. Corrupt professionals usually get their payoffs from middle-class patients. Some of these have no choice but to sell property, break pension funds, or borrow money just for that purpose. Considering the distress of very sick persons, it is no wonder that they are ready to make such sacrifices for their survival.

For example, a senior heart surgeon, very much in demand and employed as department head at public medical center, was charged and found guilty of exploiting patients, accepting bribery, and malpractice. In the verdict, the judge wrote: "The accused doctor took advantage of the fact that he was a senior surgeon and that some of his patients were in severe mental distress, because they needed major surgical interventions urgently. Therefore, he requested their family members to pay him high sums of money for services that he should have rendered free of charge" (because he was a civil servant in a public hospital). The judge sentenced him to seven years in prison and ordered him to pay large fines.

More than a few doctors, everywhere, do not resist earning extra bonuses from pharmaceutical suppliers for concealed promotion of their products. One way in which this unethical cooperation functions is through the delivery of public lectures to specific kinds of patients (e.g., diabetics) on how to cope with their illnesses. Such free presentations are made by specialists who describe to the audience new medications, emphasizing their advantages over their equivalents on the market. In return for these lectures, the physicians receive "fat checks" from the pharmaceutical companies. To avoid paying taxes, some of the accomplices enjoy fully paid vacations in upscale resorts instead of cash.

Disguised advertising of specific medications or technologies takes place quite often in a variety of publications (e.g., magazines, newspapers, journals, newsletters). In them, seemingly professional articles written by medical specialists praise the wonders of certain products, at least, as is implied in the subtexts. The global diffusion of the Internet expands spread of this method of promoting such products to large populations everywhere.

A different form of corruption in the medical profession may be seen in the area of research. Numerous practitioners in medical centers teach at schools of medicine (i.e., university hospitals). They are eligible for academic promotion up to the rank of full professor. For that purpose, they have to provide evidence that they conduct research projects, present papers in international conferences, and publish articles in scientific journals. Obviously, the title of professor for such practitioners entails elevation of their status, prestige, power, and income. In light of these benefits, some physicians cannot resist the temptation to fake studies that they have not conducted, to publish false findings, and to gain credit for work they have not done. Occasionally they get caught and are likely to pay a heavy price for their false pretences. From our perspective here, professional corruption is first and foremost an abnormal condition of organizations. It is a plausible assumption that in so-called "knowledge-based" organizations the likelihood of this form of corruption is rather high.

Corrupt professionals erode their organizations' credibility, as well as their own profession in the eyes of the public. In democratic welfare states, they distort the principle of universal service by the public sector to all citizens, laid down by the law of the land. Like the other forms discussed here, professional corruption tends to be a "contagious" disease, turning into pathology with its detrimental consequences.

Conclusion

Organizations of most kinds can be afflicted by the corruption of their members. They have always been targets of individuals and groups aspiring to maximize their own gains at the expense of the organization and contrary to their goals and tasks. No wonder then that corruption in its various forms is a pathological phenomenon since it causes direct and indirect damage to the victim organizations. In certain severe cases, corruption brings about the end of the organization.

Corruption goes hand in hand with greed. The love of money and the drive to obtain more and more of it, no matter what, and as fast as possible, breeds corrupt members of organizations—employees, partners, and executives. The pursuit of success, as displayed by material symbols of status and life style, intensifies the greed motive among members of organizations.

While rank-and-file employees on the lowest rungs of the organization usually steal small sums of money and modest valuables, executives at the top grab large sums by sophisticated methods. The former tend to justify their corrupt acts as redress of injustice, whereas the latter excuse their thefts as necessitated by the burden of their expensive lifestyle. Whatever the reasons, the greed factor plays a major role in individuals' misconduct. Greed-driven corruption is a built-in problem in public service organizations as well as in private enterprises, and it is very hard to solve or cure.

The most common form of corruption is probably political. Political corruption is essentially a secret deal between a candidate for high office and some stakeholder. Such illegitimate deals provide the candidate political support and finances, in return for acts in the corridors of power advantageous to the stakeholder's interests. Stakeholders who frequently engage in such corrupt deals include major entrepreneurs, corporation executives, labor union leaders, and even organized crime bosses. These are *quid pro quo* arrangements that link money and power in the most corrupt sense.

Many organizations are forced to endure the damages caused by individuals, groups, and sects that pursue religious, social, or political goals by unethical and illegal means. Although it involves conscientious men and women, ideology-driven corruption is as detrimental to organizations as its other forms.

Malpractice denotes injurious conduct by an individual acting in an official or professional capacity, such as a doctor, a lawyer, an accountant, an engineer, or a scientist. Misconduct by such professionals is essentially corruption when doctors, attorneys, researchers, and the like employ them in the public sector. Whether those corrupt professionals are motivated by the pursuit of income, power, status, or prestige, their misconduct inflicts serious damage on their workplaces.

Corruption, in its various forms, is pathological in nature. It affects organizations' strength, integrity, and legitimacy among the public. Corruption undermines the foundations on which organizations in the public sector are built. In the private sector, corruption puts their survival at risk. Eventually, corrupt organizations have to clean up and transform themselves or come to an end.

8

Corporate Crime

The last chapter dealt with the phenomenon of corruption in organizations, that is, the prevalence of unethical, immoral, and/or illegal acts committed by individual members. The purpose of such deviant activities is usually to gain higher income, status, power, and other privileges for the corrupt people at the expense of their organizations. By contrast, this chapter discusses the phenomenon of *corporate crime*.

In criminology, the concept *corporate crime* is used with regard of offenses committed by senior members of business enterprises on behalf of their organization and for its benefit (; Edelhertz, 1983; Braithwaite, 1989; Slapper and Tombs, 1999; Clinard and Yeager, 2006). Among those seniors, there are presidents of corporations, chairs of boards, executives, directors, and the like. In the present discussion, this term refers more widely to criminal activities committed by organizations of all kinds to increase their wealth, strengthen their position in their milieu, or enlarge their circle of constituencies.

Business enterprises, labor unions, political parties, voluntary associations, public agencies, and even religious institutions are likely to commit corporate crimes at one time or another. Such illegal activities are by no means one-person jobs; rather, corporate crime requires a complex apparatus that involves various professionals (e.g., accountants) who take part in those activities.

> *Corporate Crime* demonstrates that corporate lawbreaking covers a very wide range of misbehavior, much of it serious: among these violations are accounting malpractices, including false statements of corporate assets and profits; occupational safety and health hazards; unfair labor practices; the manufacture and sale of hazardous products and misleading packaging of products; abuses of competition that restrain trade such as antitrust and agreements among corporations to allocate markets; false and misleading advertising; environmental violations of air and water pollution, and illegal dumping of hazardous materials; illegal domestic political contributions and bribery of foreign officials for corporate benefits. (Clinard and Yeager, 2006:x)

In light of so many forms of offenses (Edelhertz, 1983), corporate crime presents a major threat to the surrounding society and its economy (e.g., Bakan, 2004). In the contemporary globalized economy, the damages of corporate crimes in one place are likely to spill over into other economies all over the world.

However, from the present perspective, corporate crime exerts a serious threat to the wellbeing and survival of organizations engaged in such offenses. Once a corporate crime is unveiled, the life chances of that organization deteriorate considerably. This is because clients lose their trust in a criminal provider of products or services; employees reconsider their affiliation with a dishonest employer; and investors are reluctant to put their money into a disgraced business. In this sense, corporate crime may be seen as serious organizational pathology. Like other pathologies, this one also leads to harmful consequences, possibly to the death of the organization.

Although organizational crime is actually committed by individuals, both the courts of justice as well as public opinion point to the organization at large as a criminal entity. Consequently, once such crimes are uncovered, corporations and other kinds of organizations are liable to pay a price for their misconduct. Thus, it seems instrumental to focus here on various crimes as pathogenic factors in the life of organizations.

Theoretical Perspectives

To better understand the causes and consequences of corporate crime, let us briefly summarize the main theoretical attempts to explain organizations' tendency to violate the law and commit crimes (Braithwaite, 1989a; 1989b).

One theory, known as *opportunity theory*, rests on the assumption that an organization has certain legitimate goal(s), which it strives to attain. However, when legitimate means for attaining a given goal are not feasible, an illegitimate means may serve as the alternative. Thus, the first three propositions of a theory of organizational crime might be expressed as follows:

1. Organizational crime is more likely to occur when an organization (or an organizational subunit) suffers major blockages of legitimate opportunities to achieve its goals.
2. Organizational crime is more likely to occur when illegitimate opportunities for achieving the organization's goals are available to organizational actors.

3.   Blockage of legitimate opportunities for the attainment of organizational or subunit goals foster subculture formation within an industry (Braithwaite, 1989b:338-9).

Another theory, called the *sub-cultural theory*, suggests that organizational crime is likely to occur whenever the internal culture of an organization legitimizes it. The existence of a subculture of illegitimate activities in an organization encourages members to violate the law on behalf of the organization; it also guides them on how to do it safely and effectively (Ibid.).

The third theory, *differential shaming theory*, maintains that "shaming is an expression of disproval that can be enacted in an infinite variety of verbal and nonverbal cultural forms" (Braithwaite, 1989b:340). The intention of shaming is to raise a sense of remorse and to condemn the individuals involved in offending against the law. Shaming may lead to reintegration by pointing out the unlawful act itself rather than the actor who committed it. Alternatively, shaming may lead to stigmatizing the offender, to blame and not forgive him or her for such misconduct.

Finally, *control theory* argues that most organizations abide by the law and comply with social norms because they are subject to internal social control, which supports an organizational culture of compliance that is embedded in moral norms.

Crime is less likely when compliance with the law is everybody's responsibility within the corporate culture, when the organization is 'full of antennas' and when accountability mechanisms make it known widely within the organization that certain individuals or subunits have been responsible for a crime. (Braithwaite 1989b:352)

In such organizations where control deters executives and other members from breaking the law, encouraging them to comply with internal norms to maintain their power and influence as trusted leaders (e.g., Lange, 2008).

These theories represent attempts to account for the emergence of corporate crime from different points of view. However, they do not seem to grasp the pathological nature of such misconduct and its detrimental consequences for the viability of criminal organizations in the long run.

Organizational Offenses

In light of those theories, it is useful to examine at least some of the many kinds of offenses that are frequently committed by organizations for the purpose of making more money and gaining more profits by use of unlawful means. Clinard and Yeager (2006) have categorized the wide variety of violations into six major types of corporate crime. These will be briefly addressed now.

Administrative Violations

Corporations are likely to refrain from reporting properly to tax authorities, official regulators, and various government agencies. Thus, they violate rules, regulations, and specific orders. They evade licenses and permits (e.g., trade in tobacco or alcohol), they maintain inadequate record keeping (e.g., occurrence of work accidents), they inaccurately report hazardous events (e.g., pollution discharge), and they do not comply with rules requiring businesses to register (e.g., lottery and gambling enterprises). Here is one example.

Most democratic countries require traders of military equipment to officially register, so that the trade of lethal arms is under strict control. However, quite a few arms trading companies that are engaged in this secret business evade this requirement through various manipulations. Consequently, armaments that are forbidden to be sold to foreign countries find their way to guerrilla groups, corrupt dictatorships, terrorist organizations, and drug dealers. This kind of equipment includes heavy machine-guns, rockets and missiles, and even military platforms such as armored cars, light tanks, and helicopters. Presumably, to deliver those goods, non-registered arms dealers have to produce false documents, hide behind straw companies, smuggle the arms across national borders, bribe officials, and so forth.

Financial Violations

This type of corporate crime consists of fake statements and reports to the public. For example, criminal business corporations present a falsified display of their assets and profits to the stock market so that their shares will appear more valuable than they really are. This kind of violation reflects deliberate deception of the stock exchange. Such false displays require a level of sophistication that only professional accountants are skilled enough to accomplish. Hence, corporations, intending to break the law in this way, need to work hand in hand with established accounting firms that agree to perform malpractice like this.

The cooperation between Enron Corporation and the Arthur Andersen auditing firm was perceived an example of such fraud. In 2002, the firm was convicted for obstruction of justice following its connection with the Enron scandal, as well as its faulty audits of other corporations, such as WorldCom. Andersen surrendered its auditing license and ended its operations. In 2005, the Supreme Court of the United States reversed that conviction due to serious flaws in the jury instructions. However, Andersen's reputation was seriously damaged and, hence, it lost most of its clients.

Consequently, the firm shrank from over 110,000 employees worldwide to only a couple hundred in the USA.

The Andersen case exemplifies how corporate crime imperils the life chances of organizations. Like a terminal disease, it debilitates the organizational body to the point of internal collapse. Although it is not bankrupt, the firm is doomed due to its notorious dishonesty.

The misconduct of WorldCom is another well-known example of fraudulent accounting intended to conceal the trend of decline by presenting a false image of growth and profits to inflate the low value of its stock. Once the fraud was uncovered, top management was removed and later indicted, the external audit firm (Arthur Andersen) was replaced, and an official investigation by the authorities was conducted. Eventually, WorldCom filed for bankruptcy protection, changed its name to MCI, and relocated its headquarters. This financial scandal dragged on for several years until MCI merged with Microsoft at the end of 2005.

Corporate crime in the form of financial violations at the industry level was the so-called "Banks' stock crisis" (Israel, 1983). Beginning in 1975 Israel had experienced spiraling economic inflation. To protect its financial assets, the public heavily traded in the local stock exchange. At some point, the country's five largest banks regulated the prices of their own shares by diverting their clients' savings and investments to purchase their stock. Moreover, they enticed their clients to purchase their stock by offering easy-term loans. In addition, they secretly sold and bought large amounts of their stock among themselves. Not surprisingly, stock prices consistently went up, and the public continued to buy more and more.

In 1983, the public learned to suspect the banks' manipulations, losing its trust in the "stock bubble." People began to move their investments to the foreign currency market. Consequently, the banks could not meet the increasing wave of demand because they had received credit lines, using their own stock as collateral. An economic crisis was imminent and Israel's major banks were on the verge of bankruptcy. To avoid a domino effect the stock exchange was temporarily closed and an "arrangement for the banks' stock" was agreed upon. The government actually nationalized the banks and took control over them.

When the stock exchange resumed two weeks later, those who had sold their shares had lost 17 percent of their investments. Most of the banks' shareholders waited for the day of the refund of all their money from Ministry of Finance. The government's commitment to buy back the banks' stock was estimated US $7 billion at that time. Thus, the government prevented the collapse of the banks.

Following the crisis, a national commission of inquiry was appointed. The outcome was the dismissal of the banks' CEOs and their subsequent indictment. In recent years, the banks became privatized and the government sold all of their stocks. Just recently, the banking system was compelled to implement profound changes, intended to avoid another crisis like that one.

Environmental Violations

In recent years public concern to protect the environment has increased. Evidently, the industrial sector of most countries is a major source of environmental pollution. Therefore, governments worldwide enacted a variety of laws and regulations to minimize the damage due to that sector, among others. Nevertheless, many manufacturing plants do not comply with the law, mainly due to their pursuit of profit. More and more industrial plants are required to set up sophisticated devices, such as special filters, to reduce air, soil, or water pollution. But numerous industrial plants everywhere find ways to refrain from installing such devices in order to reduce their operating costs. This is one more expression of greed-driven misconduct by organizations.

Offenses against environmental regulations may be seen as calculated risk-taking by companies, on the assumption that they are not likely to be indicted for committing crimes of that kind. Indeed, at least in some developing countries, firms that contaminate the country's natural resources are not likely to be punished by the law-enforcement authorities—neither at the individual nor at the corporate level. Elsewhere, environmental offenders are required to pay light fines or other minor penalties. Even in modern, first-world countries, the legal side of environmental protection is still rather debatable and somewhat ambiguous. Therefore, legal procedures take many years, during which industrial plants continue polluting the environment for their own profit. For example, in one area, several petrochemical plants, among others, disposed of their industrial waste by pouring it into a nearby river. After many years of abuse by those industrial plants, the river was actually dying, its aqueous life and vegetation being killed. The riverbed was saturated with poisonous materials, and its water was soaked with oils and chemicals. Obviously, it was no longer possible to fish, row, or swim in that river. Even the riverbanks become hazardous ground for hikers. Nevertheless, for years that country's navy continued to train its "frogmen" in the contaminated waters of this river. Only years later, when statistics indicated a high rate of cancer among the former naval personnel, did the long-term pollution of the river become a subject for public debate. At the end of 2001, the government decided to launch a multimillion-dollar project for the rehabilitation of the river. At the end of 2007, the river was declared clean and safe; however, the entire project was still not complete.

In addition to air pollution of the air by heavy industries like oil refineries, power plants, and chemical installations, some industries pollute the soil on which their works are built. One example is the defense industry, of which some facilities dispose of their waste by burying it deep in the ground. As a result, the groundwater, which serves for pumping fresh water, becomes contaminated with poisonous metals such as lead and fulminate of mercury. To avoid disclosure of this misconduct, such plants hide behind excuses related to national security. By this policy they endanger both the cleanliness of environment and the health of neighboring inhabitants, and they still escape justice.

It should be borne in mind, however, that business enterprises are not the only ones to blame for environmental pollution. Public agencies, such municipalities, run their sewage off into rivers, lakes, and seas. They also pile up mountains of garbage near cities, polluting the air and soil. They are often responsible for continuous leakage of crude oil, gas, and waste water from rotting underground pipelines by neither repairing nor replacing them in due time.

These and similar offenses represent pathologies, as they go on and on for a long time for selfish goals at the expense of the environment. They are truly pathological because they create an *organizational climate* that is indifferent to the damage caused to the environment. The repeated offenses are also pathological because eventually the criminal corporations will encounter the boomerang effect from the public; so they are likely to pay a heavy price for their misconduct, as high as being forced to terminate their operations.

Labor Violations

The tendency of business corporations to take advantage of poor, unemployed people as workers has evolved in most parts of the world. One form of such shameful abuse of labor may be seen in so-called "third-world" countries, mostly in Asia, where multinationals employ the local labor as a kind of modern-day slaves. Unskilled workers work ten to sixteen hours daily in return for meager wages of just a couple of dollars a day. A considerable proportion of these employees are children, young girls, and elderly men, who submit to cruel working conditions to support their poor families at subsistence level.

It is no wonder that numerous rural families in some countries (e.g., China) send their girls to the cities to work for local contractors of major international brands, which produce sports shoes, denims, casual clothing, and the like. These girls have to pay for their expenses: lodging, food, clothing, travel, and medicine. These costs are automatically deducted from their already low income, and then they must remit the remainder to their families, leaving practically nothing for themselves.

Despite the enormous volume of labor-intensive products made in those countries by this kind of slavery, there is very little protest and condemnation of such corporate crime. Presumably, the need of the first-world consumers for these goods ensures their silence. The average New York shopper who purchases a pair of tennis shoes for over $100 does not seem to consider that the worker who made them earned less than $1 in some poor, remote place.

Another violation of labor laws and regulations is the employment of foreign labor immigrants from less-developed countries in highly-developed ones. It is a well known that unemployed people in underdeveloped countries use a variety of means, legal as well as illegal, to enter into developed countries to find work. The criminal aspect of labor immigration can be seen in the miserable living conditions of the poor migrants.

Manpower companies have been making high profits by moving such migrants from their homeland to the target countries and placing them in a variety of workplaces. Since most of those labor immigrants are unskilled workers, they are compelled to take the lowliest jobs in agriculture, construction, food, and sanitary industries. They serve as the "hewers of wood and drawers of water" for the affluent society. At least in some countries they earn the lowest wages, below the minimum legal wage. The manpower firms hold the immigrants' passports, if they possess them, and charge them all manner of fees; this way they ensure their attachment to the firm, as if owned by it; their employers do not pay them fringe benefits and do not carry the costs of their lodging, medical, educational, and religious needs.

This kind of misconduct, which takes advantage of needy immigrants, is actually illegal in most Western countries. In fact, the pursuit of quick and easy profit by manpower placement companies at the expense of help-less workers constitutes a major evil of human exploitation in our times. The usual response to such accusations is this: "The standard of living of the labor immigrants in their native countries is worse than here."

However, more and more regulations attempt to constrain employers' abuse of this labor in various ways (e.g., payment of minimal wages, prohibition of trade in human beings). Immigration authorities of target countries deport many labor immigrants, sending them back to their coun-tries of origin, thus causing financial losses to their importers. Through such penalties, violations of labor laws have slowly decreased in some countries, as have the profits of the manpower companies. Nevertheless, as potential profits remain tempting, manpower companies are not likely to abandon this option of reaping huge sums by supplying cheap labor from abroad. Similarly, the employing companies need this cheap labor to remain competitive and maintain their clientele.

It is noteworthy that other industries have been following this lead by means of temporary employment of students, new residents, unskilled workers, single parents, and elderly people, paying them the lowest wages and no fringe benefits. They are hired and fired frequently to prevent them from becoming unionized, thereby stopping them from claiming compensation upon discharge. The fast food industry, security companies, and transport and porterage are notorious in this respect.

Manufacturing Violations

This type of violation pertains mainly to the quality and safety of products, correct labeling of merchandise, and providing the public with full and accurate information about the content of products.

Here is one example: A TV channel investigated a fishery company that was suspected of committing crime. The reporters used a hidden camera to film the company's employees as they replaced the original expiry date stickers with new falsified ones. The organization did this, and sold food unsafe for human consumption, to avoid discarding large amounts of fish and losing considerable income. The TV investigation discovered that this kind of deceit was not an occasional act but an ongoing policy of the firm. The fish was brought in from remote seas, so the time that passed until marketing was often too long for the fish to remain fresh. Thus, the health hazards of such a corporate crime to the public at large might be notably high. Once an epidemic infection of spoiled fish starts to spread among consumers, the fish supplying company is domed.

Quite a few manufacturers depreciate the quality of their products without due notification to neither the authorities nor the consumers. By this means, they are able to keep their prices competitive even though their products are of a lower grade. This depreciation is accomplished either by removal of some costly ingredients from the product or by simply replacing high quality materials with lower quality ones. The pharmaceutical, cosmetic, and food industries are in a better position than others to perpetrate this deception as they can change formulas in a way hardly discernable by consumers. This kind of offense is not only illegal but also immoral, as they may jeopardize consumers' health. The baby food case (described in detail elsewhere in this volume) proved that the removal of vitamin B1 from the formula caused severe disability and even death of infants fed with the unsafe product.

On the 24th of May in 2001, in the midst of a wedding celebration, when many of the guests were dancing, the third floor of a functions hall suddenly collapsed. Twenty-three guests fell to their deaths and 380 were injured. A government commission of inquiry found out that this calamity was the result of an "innovative" construction system of ceilings. The system was based on the use of soft tin and the omission of vertical steel poles to support the ceiling, critical to keep the structure stable. Although this construction system had not proved its robustness in laboratory tests, it was applied in many public buildings (e.g., schools, offices, parking structures, libraries, and shopping malls). The commission of inquiry concluded that marketing these ceilings as strong and solid structures was nothing less than a fallacious display of an unsafe product. This collapse was neither the first nor the only one. Prior to that incident, several ceilings constructed in the same way failed in various places on different occasions. The inventor of this dangerous product (and three of his partners) was indicted and sent to prison for four years. The owner company of the functions hall was ordered by the court to pay heavy fines for its culpable neglect.

Unfair Trade Practices

This category includes a wide variety of violations intended to reduce free and honest competition. Such violations take place in the form of monopolization of the market, secret agreements between competitors intended to deceive customers, and allocation of markets among competitors. They also include price fixing, price discrimination, and similar practices intended to prevent fair competition. Furthermore, corporate crime of this type consists of illegal interlocking directories, illegal mergers of companies, dishonest bids, and so forth.

In some countries, companies rendering cellular phone services tend to tie clients to them by long-term agreements. They offer package deals that require their potential customers to sign long-term contracts, which bind them for two or three years ahead. Once a customer signs the contract he or she is likely to encounter difficulties in annulling the contract. They include fines by the company for breaching the contract, delays in removing the customer from its clients' lists, and continuation of charging unlawful monthly payments for several months even though it no longer actually renders services. Considering that the majority of such customers are ordinary people who are unfamiliar with commercial contracts, the "regret function" is too high for them. Those and similar actions of cellular companies reflect the tendency of corporations to take advantage of naïve customers. Not surprisingly, they are not the only ones. Cable TV companies and wireless Internet companies find their own ways to bind clients by long-term, complicated contracts as well.

Another prevalent offense may be seen in the practice of public sector agencies to call for supposedly open tenders, whose results have actually been predetermined. Some agencies customarily circumvent the requirement to hire new employees, to purchase new material and equipment, or to select contractors by fair bids. To make sure that their preferred applicant wins the bid, they illegally furnish them inside information, they secretly advise them how to submit their tender, and they deliberately discredit the other applicants. In more extreme cases, unfavorable applicants face hidden threats, they receive false and misleading information, and they are discouraged to submit their candidacy. Bribery is given and taken in a number of such cases. Similar distortions of public tenders are usually concealed and denied as non-existent, unless they are exposed by the press or litigated in court.

No less important is false advertising of products and services. Commercial firms everywhere tend to advertise merchandise under false pretenses, claiming that the goods contain some useful qualities, which the public want. Promised results such as "health," "longevity," "safety," and "potency" are probably among the most popular in the realm of advertisement. They are based on the premise that it is difficult, if possible at all, to scientifically establish the relationship between the product and its promised utility.

The food supplements industry is a typical of such pretenses. According to the press, research findings conclude repeatedly that various dietary supplements are not useful, and some of them may be even harmful. For instance, countless people consume various vitamin capsules daily through the influence of the advertising machinery. But research studies indicate that while vitamins are beneficial when consumed as part of natural foods (e.g., fresh produce, meats, various nuts), they are apparently not so when packed as condensed supplements. Actually, prolonged consumption of some vitamin supplements may shorten the life expectancy of otherwise healthy human beings, as some experts claim.

Another example of unsubstantiated advertising may be often found in the ads of the cosmetics industry. Women consumers are assured that all kinds of facial creams will remove wrinkles from their faces. According to dermatologists, no cream is capable of performing such a miracle, only plastic surgery of one kind or another may work. Nevertheless, this industry continues to advertise a large variety of miraculous shampoos and hair conditioners, "aphrodisiac perfumes," as well as "anti-aging" products.

Considering all these kinds of corporate crime, Slapper and Tombs (1999:39) reached the following conclusion.

> The findings of Clinard and Yeager are similar to those of Sutherland, in that both studies provide clear empirical evidence that violations are widespread amongst even the largest and seemingly most 'respectable' of corporations. Other subsequent, somewhat similar, attempts to measure the incidence of corporate and organizational offending via quantitative analysis of large data sets have confirmed these albeit highly generalized conclusions.

Finally, there remains the question "how can an organization restore its legitimacy and achieve reintegration with a diverse group of stakeholders after committing a publicly known transgression?" (Pfarrer, et al., 2008:730). Pfarrer and his associates propose a four-stage model, by which such organizations can reach that reintegration and increase their chances of survival. The authors identify these stages as follows: (1) Discovery, (2) Exploration, (3) Penance, and (4) Rehabilitation. Briefly, the first stage requires the organization voluntary disclosure of internal investigation and public cooperation. The second stage requires acknowledging wrongdoing, expressing regret, accepting responsibility, offering amends, and apologizing. The third stage requires the organization to accept verdict, acknowledge that the verdict is equitable, and to serve time without resistance. In the last stage, the organization has to conduct internal changes in management, display a new ethical image and corporate responsibility, as well as present a new mission statement (Ibid., p.735, Table 1).

Conclusion

Steven Box (1983:20-22) defines corporate crime as "illegal acts of omission or commission of an individual or group of individuals in a legitimate formal organization, in accordance with the goals of that organization, which have a serious physical or economic impact on employees, consumers...the general public and other organizations" (cited in Tombs, 1995: 132). Thus, one of the most destructive pathologies in the realm of organizations is corporate crime. This type of crime contains a wide range of violations committed by business enterprises and/or government agencies. Contrary to other illegal activities, these are primarily intended to benefit the offenders' organizations. Not surprisingly, senior members of corrupt organizations submit false reports, manipulate stock values, underrate profits, and commit other unethical and unlawful activities for the sake of their organizations. Altogether, those and similar violations of the law represent an economic type of collective crime. In the business sector, private and public, such crime is intended to enhance the economic strength of the corporation.

In spite of the excuses used by the offenders, corporate crime cannot be justified for the following reasons: First, crime is crime irrespective of its motives and reasons. Second, executives and senior professionals who take part in corporate crime are hardly altruists; in most cases there is something in it for them too (e.g., profit, power, prestige). Third, corporate crime serves these offenders as a cover-up for their personal corruption or managerial incompetency. Last, corporate crime is most likely to be exposed eventually, and the consequences would be devastating for the focal organization and its members.

In light of the numerous kinds of violations of the law by organizations, they have been classified into six major types: administrative violations (e.g., failure to register as required by the law of the country), financial violations (e.g., false statements, "double bookkeeping"), environmental violations (e.g., polluting the environment), labor violations (e.g., abuse of labor immigrants), manufacturing violations (e.g., production of hazardous products), and unfair trade practices (e.g., monopolization of the market, false advertisement).

Criminologists have developed several theoretical perspectives on corporate crime. They are the opportunity theory, the subculture theory, the differential shaming theory, and the control theory. Each theory attempts to explain the conditions under which organizations are likely to follow the criminal route. Once any kind of facilitating conditions ripen, senior decision makers have to make up their mind whether or not they are ready to commit some unlawful conduct for the sake of their organization. In light of the probability of success and failure of such misconduct, corporate crime is presumably neither an accidental nor an idiosyncratic response; it is rather a rational choice made by its leaders.

The organization's offenders against laws and regulations tend to hide under the "shelter" of their organization, expecting to be protected if and when they are caught. They rely on the best legal assistance from the corporation's lawyers to save them from the long arm of the law and to escape severe sentences of the courts. In fact, they frequently claim to be only proxies of the corporation, who took the risk of offense to protect their employer at their own expense.

As the phenomenon of corporate crime is usually a repeated pattern, it resembles abnormal behavior of organizations. Like the abnormality of addiction, corporate crime leads to internal problems such as tensions and frictions among its members. Sooner or later corporate crime becomes exposed before the eye of the public. Once such misconduct is uncovered, a fatal collapse is likely to occur.

As corporate crime, in its various forms, is unethical, illegal, and immoral, it should be treated as a pathology that poisons the relationships between organizations and the public. It presents a negative model to low-ranking employees, suppliers, and contractors. Hence, it creates feelings of mistrust, hostility, and resentment, which eventually afflict the criminal organizations, so as to put their survival at risk.

9

Crises and Fixations

Organizational crisis denotes a turning point in the lifecycle of an organization. A crisis may be a sudden impairment in the functioning and performance of an organization; it may also occur after long period of malfunctioning that developed gradually until it reached a critical stage. A crisis in an organization resembles a turning point in a disease, which may lead to an acute state or to collapse.

In psychology, *crisis* refers to "any sudden interruption in the normal course of events in the life of an individual or a society that necessitates re-evaluation of modes of action and thought. This general sense of a loss of the normal foundations of day-to-day activity is the dominant connotation of the term and is broadly used" (Reber, 1987:166).

During their lifetime, organizations are likely to run into several crisis situations. External forces occur as a *random shock* or *niche erosion* and shake the normal course of events in organizations and can cause some crises. Crises may also come about as result of internal strains, caused by some inherent deficiencies and faults. Moreover, crises are quite common events in the growth process of organizations.

In general, crises threaten the wellbeing of organizations to one extent or another. In the wake of a crisis, organizations often go through processes of decline that can lead to their final dissolution. Yet, under certain circumstances, organizations are more likely to cope with their crises and come out stronger than they were prior to such events. Nevertheless, organizations waste so much energy to survive a crisis that afterwards they remain exhausted for quite some time. Given the traumatic and stressful nature of crisis, it seems useful to look at it as pathology that threatens the life of an organization, although it need not be fatal.

An organizational crisis may be a reaction to some extreme pressure from the environment (e.g., economic recession), and it is likely to develop due to some internal deficiency of the organization (e.g., bad

115

management). Analogous to human beings, organizations fall into a state of crisis due to some trigger, such as a critical event, an external or internal change, or some kind of outburst. Wars, revolutions, mergers, strikes, and boycotts represent such triggers of crises. These and similar incidents may lead to a crisis within a single organization. When such triggers are forceful and diffuse, they generate crises in entire industries, such as construction, tourism, or agriculture. The skyrocketing prices of crude oil create crises in the aviation, automobile, and transportation industries, among others.

At this point, it is should be noted that the ability of an organization to manage a crisis properly is somewhat determined by the type of crisis it encounters. Thus, different types of crisis are likely to affect the organization differently and to elicit different responses. Therefore, a correct detection and identification of the type of crisis might be crucial for the application of a proper crisis management plan.

Booth (1993:86-88) classifies organizational crises according to three main types. He calls the first type a *creeping crisis*. It is characterized by the gradual erosion of the external environment and/or by an internal process of decline. A creeping crisis might not be recognized as such by the organization's leadership, and therefore the usual response is bureaucratic in nature, namely, adherence to traditional rules and procedures and maintenance of the status quo.

The second type is called a *routinized crisis*. This type of crisis represents a periodic threat to the organization and/or a serious loss of critical resources (e.g., budget cut). In such cases, "contingency plans are prepared, which are the subject of inter-organizational bargaining. Internally, groups are alive to the threat or loss as it may affect them, and internal political clashes are frequent" (Booth, 1993:87).

The third type of crisis (unnamed) is a completely unexpected sudden threat or loss that endangers the entire organization and its survival. Due to the unexpected nature of this type of crisis, in most cases there are no pre-planned contingency programs to cope with it in an orderly manner. Therefore, crisis management takes the form of a defensive response. "After the shock has worn off, which can take a significant amount of time, a 'siege strategy' is often adopted. This entails selecting what is seen as essential to survival and reducing or abolishing other more peripheral activities" (Ibid.). However, this strategy is not likely to succeed, as it requires extensive layoffs and a great deal of conflict.

One common scenario is called the *phantom crisis*. This term denotes a situation in which members of an organization perceive a crisis where none exists. Such a crisis develops due to the misunderstanding of a situation, misinterpretation of data or due to certain fears and anxieties. "This sort of misdefinition of a situation, which is widely accepted, can lead to what amounts to a self-fulfilling prophecy. From a situation of no crisis, a major crisis can be rapidly manufactured due to one or two indicators that may be insignificant" (Ibid, p. 89).

Another perspective on the issue of organizational crisis is proposed by the organizational lifecycle paradigm. According to this theoretical approach, organizations progress from one stage to the next throughout their life span. Upon entering a new life stage, the organization encounters a new set of constraints, experiences, and related dilemmas with which it has to cope. We call this type the *maturation crisis.*

Growing organizations move through the stages of a lifecycle, and each stage is associated with specific characteristics of structure, control systems, goals, and innovation. The life cycle is a powerful concept for understanding the problems that organizations face and how managers can respond in a positive way, so as to move an organization to the next stage (Daft, 2004:330).

Lifecycle Stage Crises

Larry Greiner (1972; 1998) presented a model that consists of five phases of organizational growth: growth through *creativity,* growth through *direction,* growth through *delegation,* growth through *coordination,* and growth through *collaboration.* These are evolutionary stages, associated with both the age and the size of organizations. "It is important to note that *each phase is both an effect of the previous phase and a cause for the next phase"* (Greiner, 1972:41).

Each stage in the organization's evolution leads to a revolutionary stage, namely, a state of crisis. Thus, the creativity stage leads to the *leadership crisis,* since the founders are no longer capable of leading the growing organization in light of the problems that need to be resolved by professional managers. The second revolutionary stage occurs as a result of an *autonomy crisis,* in which lower-level managers struggle for power and demand greater autonomy vis-à-vis the top management. The next stage of growth is characterized by decentralization. Consequently, executives lose control over their diversified organization and, hence, a new *control crisis* is most likely to develop. These problems require new solutions in the form of coordination mechanisms. During this phase, formal systems of coordination are applied. "The proliferation of systems and programs begins to exceed its utility; a *red-tape crisis* is created" (Ibid, p.43). The organization is too complex to be managed by such procedures. The last phase, according to this model, is that of collaboration, which builds on a flexible and behavioral approach such as team action. Similar to the former evolutionary stages, this one, too, is likely to create the next crisis, which according to Greiner centers on the "psychological saturation" of employees.

This model has several features in common with other lifecycle patterns. The stages progress sequentially; they take place in hierarchical progression; and they involve a range of organizational activities and structures (Quinn and Cameron, 1983).

According to this model, before an organization can pass from one stage to the next, it must successfully cope with a crisis that typifies its current stage. Thus, the view of life-stage crises provides a theoretical attempt to account for the fact that organizations successfully evolve from stage to stage, going through a series of crises. In his commentary published over twenty-five years after the initial presentation of his model, Greiner (1998:64) insisted, "revolution is still inevitable."

Indeed, transitions between developmental phases do not occur naturally or smoothly, regardless of the strength of top management. All organizations appear to experience revolutionary difficulty and upheaval, and many of them, rather than continue growing, falter, plateau, fail, or get acquired. In other words, some organizations are stuck in a certain stage, unable to make the necessary transition to the next stage.

In psychology, from which these ideas were actually borrowed, the term *fixation* denotes the outcome of an unresolved crisis. Thus, "as derived from psychoanalytic theory, [fixation is] the process whereby one becomes excessively attached to (or 'fixated' on) some object or person that was appropriate for an earlier stage of development" (Reber, 1987:279).

Obviously, the fixations of organizations are not *affective* in nature like those of human beings. Nevertheless, occasionally organizations are unable to cope with some crisis during their process of growth. In such cases, organizations get fixated in ways that to some extent resemble fixations of individuals. That is, they lag behind their actual age and size. This fixation displays itself in "childish" behavior, expressed by the performance of inept rituals.

For instance, there are quite a few start-ups that are managed, quite amateurishly, by their entrepreneurs, to a point of crisis, whereby they are unable to replace the founding fathers with professional managers. Consequently, they lag behind their competitors, falling into a process of decline. Thus, incompetent management of this kind is apt to lead the young organization to its early demise (cf., Stinchcombe, 1965). Many family-owned enterprises get stuck in the entrepreneurial stage, unable to grow, due to the owners' fear of relinquishing their power and placing it in the hands of "strangers" who are not part of the family.

The *success-breeds-failure* syndrome refers to the propensity of mature, well-established organizations to stick to old-time routines and practices, despite their obsolescence. In other words, such organizations become fixated, entrenched in outmoded practices that are no longer effective (Cameron, Sutton, and Whetten, 1988; Miller, 1992; Sheaffer, Richardson, and Rosenblatt, 1998). This kind of adherence to past success turns into a major inertial force, which prevents necessary changes in the organization. Failure is most likely to occur under the guidance of executives and decision makers who maintain this attitude. Therefore, fixation in a changing environment can be regarded as a pathology, which endangers the future of an organization that has done well in the past.

About three-quarters of a century ago, a small spinning mill was established in a developing society. Gradually, that enterprise grew to become a large-scale textile concern, which produced inexpensive, simple cotton garments, initially marketed to the working class and later on to the public at large. Since those comfort garments suited the economy and culture of the society at that time very well, it became a leading brand name and a national symbol. However, with the passing of time, the population became more affluent and consequently the market sought more stylish and fashionable clothing. Due to external and internal economic problems, incompetent management, labor strikes, and change of ownership, the company fell into a process of decline and was unable to launch a successful turnaround strategy. Its products, which had been in high demand for so many years, were no longer suitable for the contemporary market. Finally, in 1985, a court of law declared the firm bankrupt and, accordingly, it was disbanded. The former plant site was transformed into a thriving shopping center. Thus, the closure indicated the demise of a symbol as well as the end of an era in that society.

Fixated organizations may survive as such despite their incompetence and their inability to continue growing. Plenty of them, mainly in the public sector, stay viable due to political interests of certain stakeholders. In the private sector, such "fixated enterprises" manage to survive as long as they are capable of "keeping their head above water." Tushman and Romanelli (1985) have suggested a different theoretical approach to the analysis of organizational change. They propose a *punctuated equi-*

librium model of organization evolution. "Organizations evolve through convergent periods punctuated by reorientations (or recreations) which demark and set bearings for the next convergent period" (Ibid., p. 171).

The so-called "metamorphosis model" assumes that the performance of organizations is influenced by the extent of their fit with the environment as well as by the consistency between their internal activities and their strategic orientation. During periods of convergence, organizations conduct incremental changes and use other means of adjustment to attain a high level of internal consistency. However, when faced with external changes or lack of internal consistency, organizations often feel compelled to either conduct radical changes, which can result in low levels of performance for a prolonged period. "Sustained low performance leads to either failure, or crisis associated with a fundamental reordering of activities and/or restatement of strategic orientation that will lead to a transformation of supporting activities" (Ibid., p.178).

Periods of convergence tend to intensify the inertial forces inside organizations; therefore, the longer those periods last, the higher the levels of turbulence and the risk of failure during the process of reorientation. That is, the crisis that emerges is actually deep-rooted and hazardous. Under such circumstances, it is necessary for the focal organization to implement a fundamental change, rather than an incremental one. Yet, a successful transformation is not very likely under these conditions. Crisis situations are characterized by turbulence, uncertainty, conflict, and even loss of direction. They usually follow prolonged periods of decline. Consequently, members of an organization distrust the competence of top managers; they become disillusioned and alienated, and develop anxieties associated with the possible loss of their jobs. As a result, they focus on their occupational survival, and begin searching for alternative employment elsewhere. In short, they suffer from *survivors' symptoms,* which are typical of employees in organizations' states of crisis, decline, downsizing, and upheavals.

In this sense, the analogy to physiological and/or psychological pathology is presumably in order here. This is because the stages of so-called "reorientation" or "re-creation," which are abnormal in nature, are comparable to periods of disease. They represent revolutionary attempts, in the form of radical changes, which involve a great risk of failure. Although some successful cases have been repeatedly cited in the literature (e.g., ATT, GE, IBM, Xerox, and Ford), there are plenty of cases of failure that occur every day, which receive scanty attention. Hence, "we know relatively little about the nature and characteristics of organizational evolution, and even less about how patterns in organization evolution discriminate between those few organizations that prosper over time, and the majority that fail" (Tushman and Romanelli, 1985:172).

Warnings and Precautions

In many cases the occurrence of crises is neither accidental nor random. On the contrary, it is quite predictable and can be identified by early-warning signals. In fact, certain kinds of organizations are crisis-prone, due to the risk of recurrent crises. They have been characterized by D'Aveni and MacMillan (1990) in two models: *crises-denial type* and *mal-adaptation type*.

> The crises-denial model suggests that managers will not change their focus of attention in response to an externally induced crisis. The model suggests causal relationship that leads managers of failing firms to ignore external crises. (D'Aveni and MacMillan, 1990:636)

The mal-adaptation model suggests that managers of low performance firms neither scan the external environment nor understand it properly. "This lack of scanning can be a crucial error because it inhibits a firm's ability to adapt to some of the most frequent and serious external threats facing failing firms, like declining demand" (D'Aveni and MacMillan, 1990:636-637).

Thus, organizational crises are predictable and, once recognized, can be circumvented well in advance, as long as the leadership notices the early warning signs on time. However, due to several reasons, the likelihood of detecting such signals and taking adequate precautions is rather low. One of the main reasons is prior success. Executives of successful organizations tend to ignore the warning signals of an impending crisis. They adhere to the effective strategies of the past, ignoring the future. This tendency is a well-known syndrome, described as "success-breeds-failure" due to its predictable outcome (Cameron, Sutton, and Whetten, 1988).

> Organizational scenes provide ample instances where past successes are interpreted by managements as evidencing adequate internal practices, competence and fortitude. These successes, in turn, often fixate managerial behavior into prevalent dangerous patterns. (Sheaffer et al., 1998:2)

Apparently, the recent failure of General Motors presents a typical case of this "success breeds failure syndrome," which was the largest corporation in the world.

In more than a few cases, managements do not interpret correctly the warning signals of economic and financial data. Such misinterpretation may occur because managers do not possess the necessary tools for deciphering mathematical and/or statistical models. It may also be due to a manager's skepticism regarding the practical utility of such information for strategy or policy formation. In some cases, managers feel misled by accountants and consultants pretending to make sense of such figures. Thus, the inability or unwillingness of executives to respond to these early warning signals with measures of precaution may create a crisis, followed by failure of the organization.

Certain organizational cultures may encourage their members to be sensitive to signals that might point to some hidden problems. However, in other organizational cultures, members learn not to pay much attention to such warning indications. A high rate of labor turnover, an unusual number of client complaints, or the recalls of deficient products are examples of such early warning signals. Disregard of these and similar patterns prevents managements from taking the necessary precautions and from searching for proper solutions to the problems. In this sense, culture plays a major role in the occurrence of organizational crises.

The disintegration of the Columbia space shuttle (February 1, 2003) illustrates the effect of NASA's culture at that time. Briefly stated, based on past successes, the people at NASA underrated risks and probable failures. The motto "we can do it" spread a sense of self-confidence despite technical, budgetary, and safety constraints. The drive to accomplish highly complicated missions had lead managers to overlook problems, deny faults, and ignore safety rules. Hence, middle managers blocked upward feedback of irregularities, saving the "bad news" from top managers. Thus, an atmosphere of compliance and conformity prevailed throughout the ranks. In light of such a culture, it is no wonder that the officers in charge of the mission ignored early warning signals and underestimated the risk of total failure. Therefore, the safety measures that were taken much after the initial warning signs had appeared were too little and too late to be effective. That which "will not happen to us" did happen indeed; in fact, it was an accident waiting to happen.

Richardson (1995:1) summarizes the "success breeds failure" symptoms as follows: "Crisis-prone organizations often exhibit behavior patterns, which are, for example, *too* selfish, *too* introverted, *too* competitive, *too* autocratic, *too* technically biased, and *too* busy and *too* secure." He makes it clear that the use of the word "too" refers to the propensity of crisis-prone organizations to over-emphasize certain qualities in the way they behave and perform their tasks.

Crisis-prone organizations are somewhat like human beings suffering from a chronic physical or mental illness. Both are likely to experience recurrent crisis events from time to time. The length, the severity of such episodes, and the remission periods between them differ from one case to another. Crises most likely occur in response to some environmental trigger effects, such as sudden changes. The ability, or inability, to adequately respond to such crises depends on certain inherent traits, or the deficiency thereof, that create a predisposition for coping with crises.

Organizations, like human beings, exhibit certain patterns of behavior, including denial or repression of early warning signals, as well as avoidance of precautionary measures altogether. Consequently, the crisis comes into effect rather soon. The analogy to human pathology is further pertinent concerning the long-term effects. Just as we know that each health-related crisis deteriorates one's overall health and places the patient at further risk, so too do recurrent crises pose a severe risk to the lifespan of a "sick" organization. In this respect, the propensity to undergo repeated crises reflects a chronic pathology, which eventually may be fatal to a crisis-prone organization. However, research findings reveal repeatedly that it is possible for organizations to avoid such terminal consequences, or at least postpone them, by applying proper crisis management plans.

Crisis Management

Crisis management is a critical part of contemporary strategic management. It is essential to ensure an organization's stability and viability for continued existence before any growth objectives can be pursued. Crisis-prone companies, especially, need greater preparedness for dealing with disasters. Effective crisis management requires a systematic and disciplined approach based on vigilance, managerial sensitivity, and a good understanding of the importance of careful planning and organizational readiness. (Chong, 2004:43)

In an attempt to synthesize the research literature, Stead and Smallman (1999) have presented a comparative summary of studies on crisis management, which consists of the main components that make up the structure of crisis. These are: (1) pre-conditions, (2) triggers, (3) crisis events, (4) recovery, and (5) learning.

Pre-conditions are sort of pathogens responsible for the occurrence of crisis events. Among them is "a nominal state of normality or an incubation of unnoticed events." Accordingly, a *trigger* refers to "specific phenomena identified by the place, time and source of their occurrence." *Crisis events* may take the form of "loosely coupled interdependent events; large-scale damage to human life and the natural environment; large economic costs; large social costs" (Ibid.). By the term *recovery,* Stead and Smallman mean, for example, "minimal procedures and operations needed to recover and conduct normal business; key activities and tasks performed to serve most important customers." Finally, *learning* refers here to a variety of outcomes (e.g., "full cultural readjustment; adequate reflection and critical examination of lessons learned") that follow the measures taken by the organization (Ibid.). In terms of learning theory, such outcomes represent either single-loop or double-loop learning (Argyris, 1982). Thus, organizational learning is the best way to cope with crises and mainly to avoid reoccurrence of future ones.

Similarly approached, Pearson and Mitroff (1993) have outlined a crisis management scheme consisting of the following five phases:

> (i) signal detection, (ii) preparation/prevention, (iii) containment/damage limitation, (iv) recovery, and (v) learning. "Signal Detection" and "Preparation/Prevention" constitute proactive types of crisis management. If done properly and if successful, these activities can prevent many crises from occurring in the first place. "Containment/Damage limitation" and "Recovery" are reactive activities carried out after a crisis has happened and together they are called "Crash Management". "The learning phase" points to the interactive aspect of crisis management. It can arise either as part of a crisis management plan in the absence of crisis or as a result of the experience of the crisis. (Elusbbaugh, Fildes, and Rose, 2004:113)

From this point of view, the integral components of crisis management plans should include detection of early warning signals and preparatory measures, which should be implemented prior to any crisis event. In other words, to avoid recurrent crises, organizations need to employ both proactive as well as reactive measures in their crisis management plans.

There are six steps that managements need to take in order to deal with crises effectively (Chong, 2004). The first step is *coping.* "To cope with a crisis is to take the bull by the horns and do whatever is necessary to reduce the damage and loss brought about by the crisis" (Ibid, p.43). For that purpose, organizations need to have crisis management plans (CMP), which specify the necessary procedures and tools that the management must implement when faced with a crisis. Whether they have prepared such a CMP or not, "the company's managers have to cope with [the crisis]. They have to put the fire out. They have to take emergency measures to protect people and all those assets that are valuable to the company, including intangible assets like goodwill and corporate image" (Chong, 2004:43).

The second step, according to this perspective, is *rethinking.* After the management has dealt with the crisis successfully, it has to spend some time learning lessons regarding the causes and consequences of that event. This means to come to certain conclusions about what went wrong, why, and under what circumstances. In effect, the task of the management is to understand what needs to be done to avoid the next occurrence of crisis.

A third step of crisis management is *initiating*. The lessons learned from the way the crisis was handled should be incorporated into a practical program that consists of preventive as well as handling measures. The top management that is responsible for this initiative feeds this information downward throughout the ranks. The fourth step in handling crisis is called *sensing*.

> The primary purpose of sensing is to catch the early warning signals of a potential crisis. This step calls for closely monitoring a company's internal and external environments. The typical strengths, weaknesses, opportunities, and threats (SWOT) analysis will help general environmental scanning and identification of alarming trends or developments that may threaten the company. If managers look hard enough, there is a good chance that they will be able to make insightful sense out of these trends and developments, thereby enabling them to identify and track important signals that presage a crisis. (Ibid.)

The fifth step in Chong's scheme is what he calls *intervening*. When the sensing procedures reveal some clear early warning signals of an impending crisis, management should proactively intervene to halt the process and, if possible, to prevent the occurrence of the crisis altogether.

Lastly, the next step is *sandbagging*. In those cases where preventive intervention avoid the crisis, then the management has no choice other than to mobilize all of its organization's members to take safeguarding actions. The pressing necessity at this stage is to prevent the collapse of the organization and to fight for its survival.

Change Follows Crisis

Organizations display reluctance to launch changes, in general, and radical changes, in particular. Change avoidance is probably due to inertial forces, which exist within organizations. These inertial forces include, among others, expenditures invested in various resources ("sunk costs"); organizational politics and power struggles; internal rules, regulations, and standards; exchange relationships with other organizations; and legal barriers that preclude entry into and exit from certain areas of activity (Hannan and Freeman, 1984).

In light of such constraints, organizations tend to compromise on frequent incremental changes. Minor changes and alterations do appease various interest groups and stakeholders and they serve to avoid clashes between them. However, they are not likely to create profound changes or to lead to transformations within the organizations. "Attempting radical structural change often threatens legitimacy; the loss of institutional support may be devastating" (Hannan and Freeman, 184:149).

On the one hand, organizational crises are painful and costly situations. On the other hand, crises are exceptional opportunities for managements to overcome resistance to changes as well as to implement fundamental ones. Actually, they call for radical changes in the organization's strategy, structure, and culture. In other words, the so-called *re-reorientation* (Tushman and Romanelli, 1985) is much more likely to take place in view of a traumatic crisis than it is under normal conditions.

Usually, it takes some time for an organization in a state of crisis to realize that it must reorient itself to embrace the new conditions in the environment. Executives, managers, and supervisors grasp the new situation and its dangers to the entire organization during this process. Fink, Beak, and Taddeo (1971) suggested a four-phase model to describe the process of organizational adaptation to a crisis situation: "...beginning with an initial period of *Shock*, then a period of *Defensive Retreat*, followed by *Acknowledgement*, and finally, by a process of *Adaptation and Change*" (Ibid.). This process closely resembles the experience of individuals who face some kind of calamity, such as a terminal disease, death of a dear kin, or a family crisis. The event usually creates a sense of shock and dismay, which persists until the individual eventually reaches a point of re-adaptation, following the introduction of a major change in one's life.

In many cases, fundamental change is the only option if the organization's leadership wishes to survive the hardships of the crisis. However, obtaining an agreement on and the implementation of such a change is a rather complicated endeavor in and of itself. It might require a negotiation process with interest groups (e.g., labor union) as well as with influential individuals (e.g., major investors). These might not be prepared to accept the burden of a risky fundamental change in the organization, due to a conflict of interests. One can easily notice this kind of negotiation whenever a governmental agency opts to become a private enterprise.

One such governmental agency in Israel, for example, had undergone a tedious process of negotiations with labor unions for several years until all parties involved had agreed upon its semi-privatization. During that period, a series of crises occurred and a great deal of income was lost due to structural inefficiency, low productivity of its personnel, and brain drain. The changes introduced by management included massive layoffs, restructuring, costs reduction, and the launching of new products.

Needless to say, strategic change in a time of crisis is quite a risky endeavor, as it creates a great deal of uncertainty with which an organization in a state of turmoil must cope. The stress among the organization's members might be too high, while their motivation to cooperate might be too low to bring about successful outcomes. Thus, although a change instituted in the wake of a crisis does not guarantee the organization's survival, it undoubtedly constitutes a more promising step than maintaining the status quo ante. However, surviving a crisis is not the solution to an organization's problems, since it does not come to grips with the causes of crisis. A change in the environment calls for a respective change in the organization.

Therefore, unless the occurrence of crisis is a rare and unforeseeable event, private and public sector organizations need to have contingency plans, which include alternative changes, designed for different types of crisis. It is plausible to assume that the greater the crisis, the greater the following change should be. Not unlike severe injuries that require damage repair by means of a surgical procedure, so too, a detrimental crisis requires critical treatment. An organizational change can be compared to a surgical maneuver. It is sometimes successful, and other times it ends in failure.

> It is true that managers cannot prepare for all kinds of crisis. However, their companies' likelihood of running into a crisis will be greatly reduced if they set their minds on pursuing their crisis management work as an inseparable part of their strategic management responsibility. Crisis management is too important to be relegated to the status of operational or tactical planning. In the final analysis, crisis management is concerned with the survival and long-term prosperity of an organization (Chong 2004:46).

Conclusion

One of the most typical phenomena in the realm of organizations is recurrent crises. All kinds of organizations are constantly vulnerable to crises, triggered by external pressures or by internal malfunctions. The concept of crisis usually refers to a turning point, following which an organization might decline or regenerate. In more than a few cases, a crisis has turned out to be a fatal event, as it causes the collapse of the focal organization. In other cases, a crisis may be an abnormal event, as it severely disrupts the regular activities of the organization.

The notion of "crisis" in organizations covers a variety of events and processes, which have been classified by scholars according to major types. The differences between them pertain to the ways in which the crises occur (e.g., sudden versus gradual), their probability of occurrence (e.g., expected versus unexpected), their mode of reappearance (e.g., periodic versus evolutional), and so forth.

Organizations may reduce the damages of crises, if not avoid them, by carefully scanning early warning signals, and by applying precautionary measures. However, leaders of organizations are quite often reluctant to implement proactive measures, because they deny, repress, or conceal the severity of a forthcoming crisis. Yet, ignoring the dangers of a crisis might lead to devastating consequences to the focal organization.

Therefore, organizations should be well prepared to manage crises with contingency plans or so-called Crisis Management Programs. Based on research findings, such programs provide guidelines on what members of the organization should do (or refrain from doing) at every phase of the crisis episode. As crises differ one from the other, so the contingencies plans should differ respectively. Management of crisis is a rather complicated and risky task, but unmanaged crises are indisputably worse in terms of the wellbeing and survival of the organization in crisis.

Effective handling of a crisis is a necessary condition for its containment, control, and the minimization of damages; nevertheless, it is not a sufficient condition for eliminating the forces that brought about the crisis. Avoidance of the next crisis requires a fundamental change of the organization's key features: strategy, structure, culture, and mode of operation. Organizational change of that magnitude is a difficult and risky endeavor, which managements are reluctant to launch. That is because radical changes affect interested stakeholders, create conflicts of interest, and provoke political struggles.

Thus, a crisis presents the opportunity to embark on a major change, which is not likely to take place under normal conditions. The greater the crisis, the greater the change it necessitates. A collective sense of emergency enables a radical measure in the form of major change to be introduced and implemented for the purpose of survival.

10

Failing and Surviving

Intuitively, one would expect failing organizations to cease their existence as viable entities, but, in fact, plenty of organizations, public as well as private ones, continue to remain operational for considerable lengths of time despite failing. This phenomenon raises some questions: (1) What does failure means in the context of organizations, other than final dissolution? (2) Under what conditions are failing organizations more likely to survive than to desist? (3) Do organizations have some kind of self-protection that resembles the immunity system of organisms? (4) What kind of external forces can support failing organizations and prevent their downfall and for what purposes? Based on the relevant literature, this chapter addresses these and related questions.

The Meaning of Failure

Despite the lack of a precise definition of failure, there is a broad consensus on the meaning of failure. Cameron et al., (1988, 1989) define it "as a deterioration in an organization's adaptation to its micro-niche and the associated reduction of resources within the organization." The result of it could be total exit from the market or turnaround (Mellahi and Wilkinson, 2004:22).

Following this conception of failure, total exit is only one possibility. Failing organizations may recover and become successful once again. However, we should bear in mind that such a turnaround might be just temporary, until the occurrence of the next failure. That is to say, some organizations have built-in, internal deficiencies that make complete recovery unlikely. Following the analogy used in this volume, failure resembles a terminal illness, which might have some remission periods followed by states of aggravation leading to the organization's final demise.

The concept of "adaptation," as borrowed from Biology, means suitability. The Oxford Dictionary of Science defines adaptation as "any change in the structure or functioning of an organism that makes it better suited to its environment." In the realm of organizations, "adaptation is interpreted to mean a change in a significant attribute of the organization... This is represented as a change in the organization's form" (Levinthal, 1997:934).

The notion of failure as "mal-adaptation" primarily means the inability of an organization to fit itself to the immediate environment, or to the particular niche in which it exists and operates. Practically, one consequence of failure in terms of fit is the lessening capability of an organization to deliver its goods in suitable quantity, quality, price, and reliability. In this sense, organizations, whether private or public, fail to the extent that they cannot meet market standards. In such cases, the failing organizations suffer from diminishing resources, such as income, materials, labor, and energy. Unless a failing organization is reduced to the point at which functioning is no longer possible anymore, it may survive the hardships of failure. Indeed, many organizations do survive in this fashion for quite some time, due to reasons discussed in this chapter.

The focus on the output of organizations, measured in terms of delivered goods and services (i.e., effectiveness), does not necessarily require dealing with the controversial issue of organizational goals in this context. Failure (and success for that matter), then, can be assessed according to concrete criteria rather than in abstract terms. Failure can be assessed also in terms of inputs (i.e., efficiency), that is, the extent to which the total on the "bottom line" is positive. In this sense, failing organizations are those that cannot balance their expenditure with their income, since they spend more than they can afford, given the value of their returns. From the present viewpoint, failure is like an acute illness. It may be temporary and curable, or chronic and terminal. Regardless of its prognosis, it displays certain symptoms.

> Symptoms of organizational failure include shrinking financial resources (Cameron, 1983), negative profitability (D'Aveni, 1989; Hambrick and D'Aveni, 1988), a loss of legitimacy (Benson, 1975), shrinking market (Harrigan, 1982), exit from international markets (Burt, et al., 2002; Jackson, et al., 2005) and severe market erosion (Mellahi, et al.. 2002; Starbuck, et al., 1978). (Ibid.)

Most of these symptoms are typical to business firms, which were established with the intent of accumulating profits for their owners. However, not-for-profit organizations (e.g., governmental agencies, voluntary associations, public institutes) are likely to fail as well. Symptoms of failure include, among others, desertion of members, budgetary cuts, shrinking donations, a decline in reputation, and even hostility of the public. Although failing public organizations have better chances of survival, in general and for longer periods than private ones, they may have to bear a stigma of failure, which damages their credibility vis á vis their constituencies.

The likelihood that an organization may fail, temporarily or fatally, is related to disturbances from two major contexts: outside the organization and inside it. The external setting imposes severe pressures on the organization, which come either suddenly, as random shock (e.g., natural disaster, economic crisis, political upheaval), or gradually, in the form of niche erosion (e.g., tough competition, shrinking demand, new technologies). The internal setting can lead the organization to failure because of incompetent management, structural inertia, or cultural rigidity.

The literature reveals that at least a dozen variables affect the likelihood of organizations to fail. The list includes several kinds of variables, such as regulatory changes (environmental), the age and size of organizations (ecological), past performance (organizational), and managerial perceptions (psychological). Failures were determined, in those studies, in terms of the organizations' death in one way or another (Mellahi and Wilkinson, 2004).

Regardless the causes of failure, the leaders of failing organizations erroneously engage in modes of behavior that are maladaptive (D'Aveni and McMillan, 1990). These patterns of behavior indicate denial of the severity of the situation, underrating of "bad news," adherence to past routines, and reluctance to initiate necessary changes. These and similar behavior patterns exacerbate the situation and they make the decline even more pronounced.

Following the present interpretation of failure, and to avoid confusion, it is important to distinguish between what is meant by *failure* and *death* here. One definition of the latter concept follows:

> I define *organizational death* as the substantial loss of customers, clients, and market value that causes an organization to cease its operations in its current form, relinquish its existing organizational identity and the ability to self-govern. (Hamilton, 2006:329)

Thus, while failure is reversible, death is not. This distinction allows us to deal with the survival of failing organizations as an alternative to their death. However, failure that persists represents a pathology that entails all kinds of operational difficulties as well as actual damage to the organization and its stakeholders.

Surviving Failure

Failing organizations are most likely to reach their demise one way or another. Nonetheless, plenty of failing organizations everywhere manage to survive despite such bouts of failures. Regardless of the burden of various liabilities, these organizations continue to function as if they were successful. Some of them carry a heavy financial deficit; others "bleed" due to excessive expenditure; and there are failing organizations that amass superfluous goods, since they are unable to deliver them to suitable markets.

Dependability

To understand this abnormal failure-survival state of affairs, it seems necessary to look at it from a longitudinal perspective. For instance, seen from Agency Theory point of view, the connection between debtor and creditor organizations (e.g., banks) represents a long-term exchange relationship (D'Aveni, 1989). Since creditors have a strong interest in protecting their investment and making a profit on it, they tend to take actions to circumvent the bankruptcy of their debtors. First, they want to make sure that their debtor is "dependable." "This is done by hiring a prestigious top management team composed of highly educated and well connected people. Maintaining low leverage and high liquidity also contribute to this end" (Ibid., p. 1123). These signals of managerial prestige and financial health avoid the need for bankruptcy, even in a state of temporary failure. However, in the longer run, the "dependability" level of a failing organization declines until it reaches a minimal (acceptable) level, below which it is compelled to declare bankruptcy.

This cut-off line serves as a final constraint on organizations' freedom to assume short-term risks that, in turn, decrease their dependability. As long as they stay above that specific "threshold," they can remain dependable and therefore viable. Creditors and executives (as well as other stakeholders) would not agree to compromise their major interests, such as income, career, and reputation, for the sake of partnership with a failing organization that proves undependable. Hence, "the dependability model treats bankruptcy as a sociological phenomenon: the evaporation of the consensus of two key stakeholders" (Ibid., p. 1134). The concept of dependability, then, suggests an explanation of certain social conditions that enable organizations to survive, up to a certain point, in spite of their failure.

Legitimacy

A widely shared acceptance and appraisal is essential for the survival of organizations, in general, and for those in a state of failure, in particular. "Legitimacy is defined as a generalized perception or assumption that the actions of an entity are desirable, proper, or appropriate within some socially constructed system of norms, values, beliefs, and definitions" (Suchman, 1995:574). An organization is legitimate as long its activities and its outputs are in line with the social norms and values of the society within which it is embedded. Thus, "legitimacy is thought to influence the life chances of organizations by affecting the organization's ability to garner important resources, such as capital and personnel, needed for organizational survival (Dowling and Pfeffer, 1975; Rao, 1994; Suchman, 1995; Zyglidopoulos, 2003)" (Hamilton, 2006:332).

Thus, failing organizations are most likely to survive, although under much harsher conditions, as long as they have gained legitimacy and can enjoy its benefits. In situations of failure, the failing organization can still maintain its legitimacy if its top management employs normative means to pull out of the situation and turn it around. In contrast, the use of measures that are unethical, illegal, or immoral would cause a loss of legitimacy and probably lead to the organization's demise.

It is worth noting here that the issue of legitimacy is much more crucial in the domain of public and not-for-profit organizations than it is in the realm of business enterprises. This is because legitimacy is essential for organizations that depend on taxpayers' money and/or philanthropic donations for their survival and, therefore, are exposed to greater scrutiny of the public eye.

To ensure continual legitimacy, then, organizations of all kinds have to build it, maintain it, and be prepared to repair damaged legitimacy (Suchman, 1995). By so doing, organizations gain an important asset, which improves their survival chances, even if they fail here and there.

Demography

The theoretical perspective of population ecology points to organizations' age and size as major factors that can predict their imminent demise. The fact that young organizations are more likely to die than older ones is well supported by research findings. This trend is due to so-called *liability of newness* syndrome (Stinchcombe, 1965).

Mature organizations, in contrast, accumulate various kinds of safeguards, which extend their life expectancy. First, they gain important experience that guides them to avoid fatal mistakes (e.g., rapid expansion into unfamiliar territories). Second, they enjoy the benefits of their *social capital* (e.g., interorganizational connections). Third, they rely on their past successes as buffers and for gaining better competitive positions (e.g., for entrance into a new market).

Thus, mature failing organizations can better withstand the hardships that such episodes of failure entail (e.g., creditors' claims, clients' complaints) and, hence, they often do manage to survive despite the hazardous situation. With the passage of time, the performance of such organizations stabilizes, as they learn lessons from their failure. Consequently, they become more reliable and more accountable entities in the eyes of stakeholders such as investors, clients, and the like.

Repeat failures by veteran organizations, however, may send different signals to stakeholders, namely, that these organizations suffer from the *liability of aging* (Adizes, 1988), that is, they display symptoms of exhaustion, inertia, and frailness. These organizations, then, are not likely to survive for long.

Like the age factor, organizational survival is also associated with the size factor. Small-scale organizations have lower chances of survival than do large-scale ones. The latter's longevity stems mainly from the power of massive participants (e.g., members, employees, clients) as well as from the volume of their financial assets. In other words, they enjoy the advantages of scale.

Large organizations benefit from higher survival rates due to the abundance of resources, public legitimacy, political ties, and economic power. The strength of large organizations enables them better absorption of actual losses and superior resistance to external threats compared to the abilities of small organizations.

It appears that giant corporations, for instance, are not likely to dissolve even in times of failure; nevertheless, some of them do occasionally go bankrupt (e.g., GM). Their enormous economic assets, strong political support, and masses of clients enable them to overcome huge losses, to downsize when necessary, and to reorient themselves vis à vis changing markets (e.g., HP, EDS). It seems that it requires catastrophic events, like the last global economic crisis, to bring about the collapse of such corporations.

Likewise, large military organizations can suffer serious defeats in the battlefield and survive those failures, badly hurt though they might be, unless they are physically demolished by the enemy. Their rich reservoir of resources: command, combat manpower, armament, and infrastructure enable them to recover quite quickly and proceed to the next encounter. It is quite likely that, under similar circumstances, any small army would be wiped out.

However, natural disasters (e.g., Hurricane Katrina), profound corruption (e.g., Enron), or major corporate crimes (e.g., Arthur Anderson) may be powerful enough to destroy even large-scale corporations. The 2008-9 economic crisis proved so devastating that even giant corporations, probably the richest in the world, failed (e.g., Merrill Lynch, AIG) and collapsed in no time (e.g., Lehman Brothers). In the era of globalization, a major failure in one place is likely to create a "domino effect" worldwide. Apparently, no organization of any kind is immune in the end.

Ownership

Another contextual factor that plays a role in the survival of failing organizations is the type of ownership. From the viewpoint of owners and shareholders, a business enterprise—regardless of its kind—justifies its existence as long as it is profitable. Investors in business tolerate losses for only a limited time, the span of which depends on specific circumstances. An enterprise that proves unprofitable for a prolonged time, however, cannot be maintained by its owners. Other flaws, such as structural inefficiency, professional obsolescence, erroneous strategy, and shrinking market share make the failure even worse. In such cases, the business organization is most likely to be sold, merged, or declared bankrupt.

On the other hand, public sector organizations such as state-owned agencies have much better chances of survival, even if they actually fail to properly render the services that they are expected to deliver. The following examples, which are quite typical in various countries, illustrate a number of such failing public organizations. There are national collection agencies, for instance, that account for only a small fraction of income tax from the labor force. Other types of governmental agencies install and operate inefficient postal and telecommunication services, such that there is a waiting period of several years before a citizen can obtain a landline telephone. There are municipal organizations that fail to effectively run public railway or bus systems. In some countries, state-owned monopolistic companies, which are responsible for the supply of basic energy resources to the citizens (i.e., electricity, natural gas, water) fail to render these services with any regularity. As a result, consumers suffer from frequent disruptions and interruptions in the flow of such basic resources. Thus, plenty of failing public agencies continue to survive, and their survival is actually enabled by several factors, such as political actors, the law, official regulators, and strong labor unions.

Nonetheless, public sector organizations that fail to "deliver the goods" work under abnormal conditions and, hence, experience a great deal of external pressures. These pressures come in the form of citizens' complaints, petitions, pleas to legislators, as well as the overt expression of hostile opinions by the mass media and proposals to turn these public services into private enterprises. Occasionally, reactions to the failures of public organizations include acts of violence committed by frustrated individuals or during disorderly demonstrations of interest groups.

Internally, the failing of public agencies elicits intensive conflicts among members and between managers, which often leads to the scapegoating of high-ranking officials and passing the blame back and forth from one department to another. Thus, although these failing organizations do survive, they actually suffer from a painful and—to some extent—humiliating pathological state of affairs both in the public arena and from within.

Permanent Failure

Efficient performance is only one—and not necessarily the most important—determinant of organizational survival. In other words, we are surrounded by organizations whose failure to achieve their proclaimed goals is neither temporary nor aberrant, but chronic and structurally determined. (DiMaggio, 1989:9)

Organizations that are in an ongoing state of failure suffer from *permanent failure*. It is somewhat like a chronic disease, reflecting an abnormal situation that needs to be explained.

Meyer and Zucker (1989) made an attempt to provide a theory that would address this phenomenon. According to their viewpoint, permanent failure characterizes organizations that persist even though they perform poorly for a long time. The notion of *performance* in this context should be determined and practically measured using primarily the well-known concept of *efficiency* (i.e. input/output ratio). The concept of *persistence* refers to the maintenance of those organizations as operating systems, despite their low performance. "Permanent failure sets in when there is little expectation that efficient and effective conduct will be restored (or, to use different language, that recuperation will take place), yet there is little disruption of existing organizational patterns" (Meyer and Zucker, 1989:45).

To begin with, some kinds of public agencies and state-owned institutes are inefficient in economic terms but nonetheless continue to be active, although unchanged, for long periods. In every country, one can find organizations such as public hospitals, public colleges and universities, public transportation companies (e.g., railways, national airlines, and municipal bus systems), state-owned defense industries, as well as various artistic institutes. These, as well as others, are often permanently failing organizations, which nevertheless are maintained by governmental subsidies.

However, should a government decide to privatize a permanently failing organization of any kind, it is likely to encounter resistance on the part of the employees. If the employees are represented by a strong and militant labor union, the government may find it very difficult to impose its policy, and therefore the organization is likely to remain public and be maintained by the taxpayer's money.

Civil servants often resist privatization of their public workplace, driven by the following motives: (1) a desire to maintain employees' present income levels; (2) concern for pension plans and other fringe benefits; (3) fear of downsizing, massive layoffs, and the likelihood of unemployment; and (4) reluctance to work much harder for profit-oriented organizations under private ownership. In light of such resistance, organizational transformation by means of privatization depends on prior agreement between the top management and the employees' representatives. The formulation of such an agreement might take several years and in some cases much longer than that.

The following example illustrates this situation. An electricity company, which is a state-owned monopoly, is the sole producer and supplier of electricity for an entire country. This enterprise has accumulated enormous debts, its profitability is rather poor, and its labor costs are high. Had it been a private business, it would have been compelled to change owners and undergo a profound transformation.

However, as long as the company remains a national provider of electricity, it persists despite its low performance. The employees have a powerful labor union, which has made it possible for them to obtain higher income levels and better fringe benefits than those of any other employee group in the country. Thus, the average monthly salary in that company is about 40 percent higher than the average salary of other employees in the labor force with similar education, skill, and work experience.

In addition to a rich basket of fringe benefits that the employees receive, they enjoy the privilege of free electricity consumption. This benefit alone costs the company, or rather the consumers who pay the bills, millions of dollars yearly. To offset its poor profitability, the company quite often requests that legislators raise the fares for electricity instead of cutting its excessive expenditure.

To ensure the persistence of the company as it is, its union resists repeated attempts at privatization and reorganization. Actually, the employees do their utmost to prevent competition. In addition to the employees as prime beneficiaries, there are other stakeholders (e.g., The General Federation of Labor, politicians, contractors, and suppliers), who prefer to keep the status quo, in spite of the company's deficiencies. This way, they and other stakeholders continue to enjoy the benefits provided them by this enterprise. In light of this power, as long as the company keeps supplying electricity regularly to the consumers (i.e., being effective), the company is likely to persist in its same inertial form.

Meyer and Zucker (1989) use the concept of *dependency* to account for the motivation of certain stakeholders to maintain organizations alive and active despite their low performance.

> Workers, who receive solely wage or salary compensation; the community, which receives only the side benefits of the firm operation in the form of employment, purchasing power, and access to goods and services produced by the firm; and the organizations using the firm's products as inputs, requiring the firm's services, or selling their products to the firm, are in a position of dependency and therefore have the motivation to support the maintenance of the firm apart from its efficiency and resulting performance. (Ibid., p. 93)

Such *dependent actors* have very few alternative sources of benefits, if any at all, to substitute for those provided by the focal firm (e.g., income, jobs, materials, and products). Hence, their prime motive is to secure a continual flow of such benefits irrespective of the firm's performance. In other words, their prime interest is to maintain the organization that sustains their dependency. Thus, by ignoring performance issues, these agents push the organization to a state of permanent failure. However, to realize this goal, dependent actors, as such, must have the power to impose their will upon the organization.

To ensure their power and influence, these actors can join forces with other interest groups, form ad hoc coalitions, and use them to initiate militant acts such as labor or consumers' strikes, demonstrations, petitions, and the like. Alternatively, they may be able to influence politicians and legislators to endorse their struggle, and to convince the court of law that the organization's role as supplier of particular goods and services is essential for the welfare of the public.

In cases in which these actors are not able to exert power over the organization's owners, they should be able to negotiate with other stakeholders (e.g., creditors, shareholders) the terms of recovery from such state of anomaly and the risk of demise. To do so, these dependent actors employ various types of *political games* with their opponents (cf., Mintzberg, 1983; Samuel, 2005). Using these kinds of politics, they attempt to maximize their own utility in return for their consenting to a *reorientation* of the organization (cf., Tushman and Romanelli, 1985). This strategy may secure their continual employment for a certain period, early retirement compensation, and/or assurance of the viability of their pension plans after the change takes place.

In quite a few countries, there are small towns, many of them located in peripheral regions, which are actually "company towns." That is, a considerable proportion of their inhabitants work for one manufacturing plant or a single mining company. Such plants are frequently low-tech businesses that require mostly semi-skilled, local employees. Due to internal or external reasons, the performance of some of these enterprises deteriorates to a point of inefficiency.

To avoid permanent failure and stop the financial bleeding, the owners tend to close down the plant or mine, disband it, or relocate it elsewhere. An act of closure might turn a small "company town" into a "ghost town." It is no wonder, then, that practically the entire population of that town tends to commit all kinds of desperate actions to prevent the loss of their major source of income. In response to various pressures, such as the rallying support of labor unions, and favorable public opinion, the central government is compelled to provide some financial help to such failing organizations. Although not a frequent occurrence, the government's subsequent intervention in the affairs of private businesses in these cases stems from political and social considerations, rather than from economic ones.

However, in some cases, it might take years for a failing organization in a remote and rather weak town to turnaround and restore its performance, if at all. These types of firms become dependent on public aid, leaning entirely on the taxpayer's money, but persevering nonetheless. As long as the firm continues to function, regardless of its inefficiency, most of its stakeholders find it worthwhile to maintain it, each for its different reasons.

Apparently, public-sector organizations are more likely to persist, regardless of their inefficient performance, as compared to the private-sector ones. Usually, the former are not-for-profit entities and their utility in many cases is rather vague. Governmental agencies enjoy annual and long-term budgets, which sustain them (e.g., Police force). Regardless of their actual performance, the taxpayer's money maintains a large variety of public agencies and enterprises year after year, because of their valuable contribution to society.

It is not surprising then that public sector organizations tend to drift towards a state of so-called permanent failure, since the government as well as the public prefer their persistent existence to their profitable performance. Public medical, educational, welfare and community services are well-known examples of organizations that render services to the public at large, not always in an efficient way. Nevertheless, organizations of these kinds do persist, since their services are essential to those parts of the population that cannot afford to obtain comparable services from private providers. Thus, governments, international organizations, and philanthropic funds, each for its own reasons, contribute to maintain such services without accounting for their performance.

It should be noted here that many public art museums, classical music orchestras, opera houses, and dance companies, among others, persist despite the fact that they do not balance their expenses by selling tickets to art consumers. In fact, they fail to sustain themselves in the end. In this sense, quite a few of them actually are permanently failing organizations. Therefore, they receive substantial support from central and local governances to keep them going. These organizations' contributions, both to the culture and the image of their communities, regions or nations, and their attractiveness as tourist sites make the existence of such organizations worthy of the taxpayers' investment.

In addition, community leaders, musicians, artists, college students, as well as various sponsors have a strong interest in maintaining such cultural centers in their towns. While each may have his or her own reasons, all of the agents who promote such organizations are actual or potential beneficiaries. Hence, unless an organization approaches bankruptcy or foreclosure, these interest groups are not bothered by issues of performance efficiency. They want to keep these cultural organizations alive and active, so that they may be able to benefit from them.

Although there are several differences between profit pursuing enterprises and not-for-profit organizations, between the public and the private sectors, and between state-owned and share-holding companies, they all share some similarities with regard to survival in a state of failure (see Meyer and Zucker, 1989).

> Language aside, however, it appears that similar processes operate across organizations of different types. Low performance (from the perspective of owners or their equivalents) triggers divergences of interests that, in turn, block change. Initial low

performance is thus transformed to sustained low performance, or permanent failure. (Ibid., p. 113)

We should bear in mind that permanently failing organizations represent an abnormal pattern of conduct, not unlike some types of severe chronic illnesses. This state of chronic malady is characterized by symptoms of malfunction, dependence on others' continual help, inability to function by one's own means, ongoing reliance on lifesaving devices, and high vulnerability to the politics of constituents. In short, it is a pathological state of affairs, which in the end might incapacitate the organization altogether.

Conclusion

Organizations of all types always face the risk of failure. Indeed, plenty of them actually fail all of the time. According to economic theories, failing organizations are most likely to reach their demise in one way or another, eventually. However, many failing organizations surprisingly survive for quite a long time. This phenomenon needs some explanation.

Failure is not necessarily the death of the organization: an organization may fail to deliver the goods and services as expected (i.e., ineffectiveness) or, alternatively, it may deliver outputs but demonstrate inadequate performance (i.e., inefficiency). Either way, failing organizations are not likely to survive for long unless their existence is more important to their stakeholders than their performance.

At least a dozen variables have been found to bring organizations to the state of failure. These variables include environmental constraints (e.g., regulation), ecological factors (e.g., age, size), organizational measures (performance), and psychological variables (e.g., management's perceptions and attitudes). Whatever the causes may be, the way in which a failing organization copes with that situation is crucial for its survival.

One way of coping with a state of failure is transmitting signals of "dependability"; that is, convincing creditors and other claimants that the organization is now controlled by competent top management, and that it handles its financial affairs adequately. A second way of coping is to gain "legitimacy" in the eyes of its stakeholders, including the public. An organization is legitimate as long its activities and its outputs are in line with the social norms and values of the society within which it is embedded. The failing organization can still gain legitimacy to the extent that its top management employs normative means to pull out and turn around.

Failing organizations can overcome the liabilities of age and size by relying on their social capital, past successes, and lessons learned, all of which can be used as safeguards. Thus, mature failing organizations can better stand the entailed hardships of failure (e.g., creditors' claims, clients' complains) and, hence, they do survive in spite of their hazardous situation. As for size, small-scale organizations have lower chances of survival than do large-scale ones. The longevity of large organizations stems mainly from the power accrued by a massive number of participants (e.g., members, employees, clients), that is, through the advantage of "large numbers." However, the 2008-9 economic crises in the U.S. and elsewhere revealed that even the largest banks and giant financial corporations are by no means immune to failure.

Everywhere, there are organizations of various types that survive for long periods even though they continually fail with no prospect of their recovery in the foreseen future. The organizations display an odd combination of low performance and high persistence, which turns them into a state of "permanently failing organizations." The concept of persistence in this context refers to the maintenance of these organizations as operating systems, despite their low performance, that is, poor organizational efficiency.

Permanent failure becomes possible whenever some of the organization's stakeholders have a greater interest in its persistence than in its performance. These stakeholders, whether individuals, groups, or organizations, are in fact dependent actors; that is, they are in need of the focal organization's goods and services, or they want to extract other kinds of benefits from its existence, such as jobs. However, these dependent actors are able to realize their interests only to the extent that they have the power to influence the owners, or the equivalent authorities in the public sector, to keep the organization alive regardless of its performance.

Given that some of these organizations render services on a not-for-profit basis, they are often more susceptible to public opinion than to the efficiency of their operations and, as a result, they are more likely to survive despite their poor performance than are for-profit providers of similar services.

Thus, many public sector organizations keep going regardless of their inefficient performance; their income is smaller than their expenditure, and not infrequently, they lose considerable sums of money due to employee or management corruption. Therefore, their maintenance usually requires the financial help of the central and/or local governments. To justify the necessity of keeping these public sector organizations alive, political leaders rely on ideological, legal, social, and cultural values that coincide with their own beliefs and interests. In a different political climate, however, these agencies and enterprises are less likely to survive, since they are the first ones to be privatized or transformed.

In sum, organizations of all kinds are more likely to fail than to die. Failure might be disastrous under certain conditions, but it might be containable and tolerable under different ones. Plenty of organizations fail but recover from their failure due to the application of proper measures. Others survive for a considerable length of time regardless of their ongoing failure. Failure, like an illness, is by no means a normal situation and, therefore, needs recovery as soon as possible. However, like chronic illness, permanent failure is not a curable pathology, and hence it requires the application of measures different from the common ones. These are addressed in the next chapter, the last of this volume.

11

Disbandment and Closure

Among declining organizations, some reach a point of no return, at which death is imminent (cf., Weitzel and Jonsson 1989). In such cases, the organization undergoes an extended process of dying, rather than a brief event as is characteristic in cases of a sudden and unexpected mortal blow ("random shock"). Sutton (1987) clarifies the meaning of the death of an organization, as compared to the death of a living organism.

> When a biological system dies, so do all of its components (except in rare cases such as organ transplants). This is not true for organizations, which have human members. Nonetheless, using the metaphor "organizational death" conveys that I studied permanent closings, which are most akin to biological deaths, and that, although social systems are not restrained by the temporal limits of biological life cycles, death is an expected occurrence in all organizational populations. (Ibid., p. 543)

As discussed in detail elsewhere in this volume, organizational death is a common occurrence—numerous organizations of all kinds and at any given time cease to operate permanently. Some are disbanded, and their main components (e.g., divisions) are handed on to other organizations. Others are merged in such a way that they lose their original form and identity. There are also organizations that collapse in the wake of natural disasters. In short, like living organisms, organizations die every day in one form or another. Thus, the law of entropy applies to social systems as well, so that all of them eventually vanish, although in different ways.

Reactions to Death

The closing down of an organization is evidently a traumatic experience for its former participants, so much so that it may be no less painful than the loss of a close relative or a dear friend (Sutton, 1987; Cunningham, 1997). Whenever work organizations have to cease their existence, the associated psychological difficulties may be even worse than those associated with the death of a loved one. The closure of such workplaces entails unemployment for many of the former employees, a fact that further reduces the distance in the analogy between human and organizational life and death (despite the obvious distinction between the two life forms).

The fact that the organization is dying requires its participants to adjust their perceptions, interpretations, and emotions to changing conditions, as unfortunate as they may be. At the beginning, members tend deny the severity of the situation. Many prefer to ignore the signals of the forthcoming death, pretending that business continues as usual. Denial of a grave situation is an unhealthy attitude, since it prevents its beholder from facing the truth with open eyes. However, many individuals do not have the courage to take such a position and, hence, they are unable to accept its full meaning.

Often workers are able to adjust to only a limited new perception, acknowledging that the organization is in a bad shape indeed. However, they consider this condition transient, a grave and unfortunate situation, but one that is likely to change for the better in the near future. That is, they see it as a reversible state of weakness or illness, which can be repaired or cured in due time. Therefore, they remain hopeful that their organization neither is nor will it become defunct in the foreseeable future. This state of mind makes it easier for employees to cope with the dying of an entity with which they have close ties.

At the third phase, the perception that death is inevitable raises feelings of rage and grief among the organization's members. "Sadness and anger are evoked when people confront impending losses, including their own death (Kubler-Ross, 1969), the death of a relative (Bowlby, 1980), and the dissolution of a personal relationship (Duck, 1982)" (Sutton, 1982:552).

With regard to organizations, the feeling of anger is a common reaction based on the assumption that somebody is responsible for the unfortunate failure. From the members' viewpoint, that "somebody" might be the owner of the organization, the top management, the state regulator, the labor union, or the employees themselves.

Feelings of sadness do not pertain exclusively to the closing organization's members. In quite a few cases, various sectors of the surrounding society or community share this emotional reaction. These are most likely investors, customers, suppliers, partners, and other stakeholders. However, this event may invoke a similar emotional response in people who have no personal interest in the particular organization, such as uninvolved citizens who feel sorrow with the closure of any public service (e.g., school, museum, theater, or hospital), the destruction of a symbolic historical site (e.g., an old railway station), or a national institution (e.g., mint, archive).

Thus, "feelings of sadness and anger in all these situations mean that people are beginning to accept that a loss will occur" (Sutton, 1987:552). "In this sequence of events, members first think of their organizations as permanent, then temporary, and finally as defunct" (Cunningham, 1997:474).

Members of dying organizations who are optimistic have better chances of connecting with alternative organizations once their present ones have become defunct. In the case of workplace, optimistic individuals are more likely than their colleagues to obtain employment elsewhere, especially if the latter refuse to accept the fact of the final termination of their workplace. In short, the former are better adjusted than the latter.

The process of coping with death does not necessarily unfold in a linear sequence as just described. Individuals' thoughts and emotions may shift back and forth in a somewhat chaotic manner. Hence, instead of analyzing people's process of mourning in terms of phases or stages, it might be more accurate to refer to "reactions" in describing the process of coping with organizational death.

The Countdown Effect

Evidence collected from various case studies repeatedly reveals a surprising increase in the productivity of employees during the countdown period, that is, shortly prior to the termination of the organization's operations and its final closure (e.g., Sutton, 1987; Wigbald, 1995; Bergman and Wigbald, 1999). Bergman and Wigbald (1999) call this unexpected phenomenon the *countdown effect*.

At a first glance, one may suggest that such an improvement in workers' performance is a result of the management's policy to take advantage of the organization's grave situation. Such a change in employee output may reflect the leadership's decision to "squeeze" more from the workers by means of disciplinary measures (usually this pertains mainly to employees stationed at the shop floor). Alternatively, it is reasonable to argue that a typical management is likely to offer tempting incentive payments to motivate employees to improve their work performance significantly. The purpose of the management in the case of closing organizations would be to gain a better bargaining position.

However, the real causes of the countdown effect probably rest elsewhere.

A common feature in declining organizations seems to be that management's control over daily operations is diminishing. This is of course a consequence of the plans and/or decisions to close down...The reason for this is, we argue, that managers' and supervisors' interest in maintaining the established order at the workplace fades away in a dying organization. Future plans for the operation, including major investments, are no longer at the top of the management's agenda. (Bergman and Wigbald, 1999:344)

In light the management's disinterest and diminished control, this increase in the workers' performance is by no means a result of managerial pressure or persuasion, one way or another.

One explanation for the countdown effect suggests that the increase in productivity is a result of local initiative, creativity, and hard work, mostly of the employees stationed at the shop floor of such factories, in light of their situation, described as "management by absence." The unplanned autonomy of these workers enables them to do things that otherwise they would not have done without the explicit permission and overt encouragement of the management.

The said effect might also be an outcome of a preventive attempt to halt the process of disbandment and closure of the workplace. It is also possible to argue that the shrinkage of the organization challenges the workers to increase their work effort, assume new tasks, and accomplish the necessary goals despite of shortage of labor force (Sutton, 1987). "Greenhalgh and Sutton (1991) also launched a psychological explanation: when uncertainty about the future becomes cruel certainty, namely layoff, psychological tension is released and hard work becomes de-stressing" (Bergman and Wigbald, 1999:348).

Finally, yet no less important, the sociological explanation is also worth mentioning. The feeling that new solutions are needed in order to help improve the organization's dire situation leads the employees to join forces and work together. Such a collective effort generates sentiments of solidarity among members, and a sense of self-control of the group. These group dynamics encourage harder work and productive performance.

Regardless of its causes, and despite the improved performance and the increased productivity, by the time these changes are implemented it is usually too late to save the dying organization; recovery at such a late stage is extremely unlikely. Apparently, the pathological deficiencies that brought the organization to drift downwards to such a low and fatal point cannot be repaired at this final stage. Like a terminal illness in an organism, sick organizations also reach a point of no return. The improved performance witnessed at this late stage is more likely to ameliorate the feelings of the organization's members than to revive the dying organization.

Disbanding and Reconnecting

Once members of an organization are officially and unequivocally informed that the organization is going to close down, the processes of disbanding and reconnecting actually begins. A study of organizational death (Sutton, 1983; 1987) revealed several interesting findings about the process of disbanding defunct organizations.

One finding was that the organizations' leaders have a strong influence over the ways that members perceive the death of their organization. Members' reactions to the forthcoming closure of their organization differ depending on the manner and source by which this information was obtained. If the management furnished a formal announcement, the fact is likely to be met with a greater degree of acceptance than if the information arrived through rumor and gossip.

It was also shown that employees usually recognize the legitimate authority of the management to close and disband the failing workplace, despite the negative consequences and unpleasantness it causes them. Although employees may feel enraged in response to the management's decision to close, nevertheless, they cannot repudiate its prerogative to do so. However, in some countries employees, in general, and labor unions, in particular, may choose to challenge that decision in various ways, in an attempt to improve their severance benefits.

Once employees are informed that their organization is no longer viable, they work harder than in the past to prevent or postpone its final demise, perhaps as a response to what they perceive as a challenge. As described above, in many cases, the outcome is an unexpected increase in labor performance and improved productivity in the final stage of the organization's life.

Following the announcement of closure, the management is expected to take responsibility for the task of disbanding the organization. In some cases, however, the remaining employees do the job of disbanding its components, while they search for ways to reconnecting themselves and others to alternative workplaces. This process is likely to take place in dying organizations in which the management and the employees have reached an agreement on the terms of departure. Such cooperation is not likely to take place if unresolved conflicts, disagreements, and power struggles are left to simmer until the final termination stage. In these cases, talented employees tend to depart from the organization and place themselves in other jobs before the process of disbanding is completed (Sutton, 1987). Similar behavior is typical also in downsizing processes, in which the best employees choose to detach themselves voluntarily from the shrinking organization at an early phase, as they seek to connect with other workplaces. The common proverb, "rats desert a sinking ship," illustrates this phenomenon quite well.

It should be noted that the act of disbandment encompasses managers and low-ranking employees; organizational settings, installations, instruments, and a variety of objects; as well as customers, suppliers, contractors, and other partners.

Nowadays, many organizations that conduct massive downsizing, as well as those that are compelled to close down, employ qualified teams to take charge of placing the organization's employees in alternative workplaces. Such placements may be in other subsidiaries of the parent corporation, they may require relocation to other communities or parts of the country, and they may include positions in outsourcing agencies. In a few cases, the closing organization has helped individuals or groups set up their own startup organizations.

An arrangement must be found for transferring installations of production lines, laboratories, computer centers, or warehouses into the hands of other organizations. Major subunits or divisions are likely to bet merged into or acquired by other corporations. Other physical objects, such as office equipment or work tools, are often sold and removed from the premises.

Most often, the closing organization advises its clients, suppliers, and contractors to take their business to other organizations capable of supplying similar products and/or services, and assists them in connecting with organizations from which they can purchase the materials and services. Such reconnection not only makes it easier for the stakeholders to continue their business, but it also serves to reduce the liabilities of the dying organization.

It was also observed that when an authorized agent unequivocally announces the death of the organization, farewell ceremonies may be held as members of the organization take their leave. As rites of passage, those ceremonies may take any form, ranging from a brief departure with a simple handshake to a ceremonial dinner at which souvenirs are distributed among honored attendees. At last, as the disbandment process draws to an end, reconnection attempts continue in various domains.

It is important to note that Sutton's model applies to a specific kind of organizational death. "The process of organizational death proposed here seems to best describe unambiguous organizational deaths that are announced in advance, those in which the organizations are dismantled through the efforts of their members, and those not characterized by severe conflict over the distribution of resources and obligations" (Ibid., abstract).

However, Sutton's pioneering study was published over twenty years ago; since then, students of organizations have had ample opportunity to learn from numerous terminations that, at least in some countries, organizations on the verge of closure evoke furious conflicts, vocal protestations, sabotage attempts, and court appeals. Hence, there may be little consensus on how to disband the organization's assets and how to reconnect them to other organizations. Employees may refuse to help, managers may shift their leadership conduct to a mode of laissez-faire, and other stakeholders (e.g., creditors, suppliers) may exert strong pressures upon the organization's board of directors and its chief executive officer to attend to their interests.

Managing Dying Organizations

Except in the case of a sudden crash, the demise of an organization usually comes at the end of a decline process that may have continued for quite some time. The managing of decline processes (discussed in another chapter) differs from the management of dying processes. The former represents attempts intended to prevent death, whereas the latter refers to the performance of tasks intended to bring the dying organization to its end. As these processes are associated with two different stages and different goals, they also require the use of different tactics.

The analogy of human illnesses may be in order here. A declining organization is typically in a state that resembles that of a sick person. Both the sick individual and the declining organization suffer from insufficient resources and lesser energy, resulting in impaired performance. Both need the help of outside experts, but they must make the proper decisions that may lead to their recovery and enable them to return to their normal state of affairs. Likewise, a dying organization seems to resemble a dying person. Both are on the verge of death, and their demise is apparently imminent. Thus, they both have reached a situation that differs from that of illness—albeit a grave one (Parker-Oliver, 1999-2000). Therefore, just as a human being needs constant and exceptional care in the final stages before the point of a hopefully peaceful death, so does a dying organization. That is, the death processes needs to be managed.

Sutton (1983:398) specifies, "eight tasks typically required for the management of organizational death," which are presented in the following list.

1. *Disbanding* and transfer of employees and other physical and organizational assets, as already discussed in detail above.
2. *Sustaining* refers to maintaining the flow of products to customers, filling standing orders, and rendering promised services.
3. *Shielding* the organization, by furnishing selective information to stakeholders.

Issuing an open announcement stating that organizational disbandment is likely to stir up a host of threatening actions and reactions from stakeholders.

To avoid such eventualities, the decision concerning closure should remain classified and hidden up until the right point in time.

4. *Informing* the stakeholders, by providing factual or symbolic information. Managers who furnish information to their subordinates about actual events help abolish rumors and speculations and reduce fears and anxieties.
5. *Blaming* others for the failure of the organization and its closure is an integral part of managing the death process and is typically expressed by those left to manage this painful stage. Thus, in stressful situations such as this one, blaming allows people to respond to their need to identify and understand the causes that led to their organization's demise.
6. *Delegating* in this context means allowing employees to take part in decisions concerning the termination of the organization's operations. Management's request for the employees' opinions, as well as granting them the autonomy to initiate necessary measures, may contribute to an easier termination process for all parties concerned.
7. *Inventing.* Since most mangers do not have prior experience in closing organizations, they need to think of new ways to do things at that stage. Unable to rely on standard managing procedures, those managing the closure must be more creative than usual (for example, by developing new manuals) despite the stressful conditions.
8. *Coping* with a stressful situation that induces fears, frustrations, and anxieties requires taking special measures in decision-making processes concerning the closure of the organization.

Measures and precautions are required for maintaining well-thought and rationally weighed decisions, despite objective and subjective obstacles. An example of a coping tactic for careful decision making is when managers assume the role of "devil's advocate" as a means for considering possible obstacles before reaching a final decision.

"Managing organizational death needs careful attention to the eight tasks described above. Yet, the completion of these tasks is complicated by some sticky dilemmas" (Sutton, 1983:403). Furthermore, it is important to bear in mind that the disintegration of an organizational entity renders a rather chaotic state of affairs. Hence, any attempt to manage an orderly, smooth, and consensual process of organizational demise is likely to encounter numerous problems. In countries such as Europe, the United Kingdom, Australia, and Israel, for example, in which employees rely on strong and militant labor unions; accomplishment of closure is a very difficult mission. Managements' decisions to close organizations (mainly for protecting the interests of the owners) may easily turn into power struggles. Employees' resistance to such acts of termination is rather persistent in times of economic recession or in peripheral regions that suffer from high rates of unemployment.

Under these and similar conditions, managing closure requires skilful negotiation and bargaining in an attempt to gain the acceptance and eventual cooperation of the stakeholders of the dying organization. To accomplish these objectives, the managing team should be granted the authority to compromise, promise compensations, and make certain concessions. Practically, such concessions have to be signed by the parties involved as part of a legally binding agreement.

To manage the process of termination effectively, the expertise of specialists in several areas (e.g., engineering, accounting, law, human resources management, and organizational consulting) are necessary. For the actual disbanding of physical installations and hardware equipment, the skills of operators will be required too. In light of the stressful nature of such processes, outside specialists are in a better position to contribute their professional knowledge impartially than are in-house professionals.

The process of organizational death, like the death of human beings, may last a considerable time—months and even years. As it is essentially a transition period, its duration is a rather crucial matter. Therefore, in managing the death process, both the pace and the implications of the pace should be considered. Figuratively, the burden of managing organizational closure can be portrayed as carrying a heavy box overflowing with objects that need to be discarded.

A hasty pace might cause one to trip, ending the process prematurely, whereas dragging on at a slow pace is likely to prove ineffective and prolong the painful process unnecessary. Thus, proper management of organizational death requires careful pacing of the process, from the moment the decision is announced until the actual closure. Incorrect pacing is likely to cause unnecessary suffering, frustration, and unrealistic hopes. It may also increase the complexity and sensitivity of such a fragile situation.

Conclusion

Organizations of various kinds eventually pass on in one way or another. Some of them reach their demise after a long process of decline. Others are victims of "random shocks" delivered in the form of natural disasters, wars and terrorist attacks, or economic crises. Dying organizations are compelled to prepare their exit by taking a series of steps and applying certain measures, which primarily consist of disbanding and reconnecting.

As might be expected, the people engaged with the dying organization, many of whom have been involved in its progress and decline for a quite a long time, are likely to express their reactions to the prospect of the forthcoming dissolution of their organization in various ways. Apparently, such reactions are not much different from people's reactions to the forthcoming death of a family member or a close friend, or from the reaction upon discovering one's own fatal condition. The imminent demise of the organization requires its members, first and foremost, to readjust themselves—psychologically as well as practically—to the changing conditions imposed on them.

One typical reaction to organizational death is denial. People simply refuse to accept the fact that the organization will not continue to exist. Another reaction is to view this grave situation as reversible, namely, to mistake it for a weakness or illness that can be repaired or cured in due time. A third kind of reaction is the perception that death is inevitable; this perception usually arouses feelings of rage and grief among members. Eventually, feelings of anger are likely to shift to feelings of sadness and melancholy. Members, as well as others who connected indirectly to the dying organization, mourn the loss of an important entity. The last reaction is the unavoidable acceptance of the forthcoming death as a permanent, albeit unfortunate, fact—a reaction that requires a new and corresponding mindset. Finally, upon closure, managers are expected to conduct farewell ceremonies for their organization's former members and other partners.

Contrary to common expectation, the performance of members in the last stage of the organization's life is most likely to improve. Employees invest much greater effort and creativity to produce higher quantity and quality of the organization's goods than they did in the past. This surprising "countdown effect" may be attributed to their need to demonstrate that the organization is not defunct yet and might be worth salvaging. It may be a response to the challenge of disbanding in circumstances marked by a shortage of work force and other means of production. This improved output may reflect the tendency of managers at this stage to increase their subordinates' autonomy, allowing them to do things their own way. The improved performance is more likely to help ameliorate the feelings of the organization's members than bring the organization back to life.

The two major tasks that need to be addressed in the process of termination are disbanding and then reconnecting the dying organization's components. Management teams are responsible for dismissing all of their employees and helping them, as much as possible, connect to other employers. Managers have to disassemble organizational divisions and to attach each one of them to different organizations. They also have to sell or give away physical objects, equipment, raw materials, and the like. Often, the most complex task is the settling of contracts and liabilities with suppliers, contractors, creditors, and long-term clients.

To ensure that the termination process is handled effectively and efficiently, it must be managed properly. To this end, the managers in charge of the death process have to accomplish a series of tasks: disbanding, sustaining, shielding, blaming, delegating, informing, inventing, and coping. Furthermore, they must be able to negotiate, bargain, and settle disputes; use the knowledge of specialists from various relevant disciplines; and pace the progress of the termination process as optimally as possible. Above all, effective management of the organizational death process requires trust in and cooperation with those involved in dismantling the organization, despite their expressions of anger and sorrow at its demise.

The main conclusion of this chapter is that organizational death is a rather long and complicated pathological process. It requires the gentle handling of emotions and anxieties as well as the careful balancing of various partners' stakes, all under highly stressful conditions. Unlike the death of human beings, it is necessary to disband the components that make up organizational system and reconnect them to systems that are more viable. In light of the chaotic nature of this situation, and given the cross pressures exerted by claimants, managing the process of closing an organization is by no means a simple and straightforward task.

12

Lessons Learned

The fact that organizations pass on sooner or later is indisputable. Most of them die because of a fatal failure, whereas others gradually dissolve after a prolonged decline. Throughout the history of human civilization, organizations of all kinds have vanished in one way or another. In addition to businesses, other kinds of organizations have evaporated, leaving behind only fading traces of their existence (e.g., empires, monarchies, armies, political parties, labor unions, and so forth).

Although organizational failure and death present interesting issues that should challenge students of organizations, they have not have received much scholarly attention. Apparently, the ethos of success in Western culture, and primarily in North American society, encourages scholars to pay much greater attention to the study of success than to that of failure.

In recent years, some students of organization and management have published theoretical models and empirical studies dealing with topics such as decline, crisis, turnaround, and the like, which they associate with failure. Some of these works pertain to broader perspectives and paradigms that relate to organizations. For instance, the "population-ecology" perspective examines the effects of demographic (e.g., age, size), and ecological (e.g., niche) factors on organizational birth and death rates. Students of another perspective, known as the "life cycle paradigm," focus on organizational growth and decline in terms of life-stage development. The "institutional" perspective associates the failure and demise of organizations with social norms and cultural values, such as the extent of their legitimacy in the public eye. The "resource dependence" perspective relates failure to the inability of organizations to secure themselves the resources vital for their maintenance.

At present, there is no encompassing theory that deals with the issue of organizations' failure—its causes and consequences. Hence, drawing upon the literature published in relevant disciplines, the present volume posits a diagnostic model of failure that identifies the major factors that account for the likelihood of failure. Notwithstanding the usefulness of the model for analytic purposes, it does not pretend to posit a general theory of failure.

The model assumes that failure may be triggered either by the external environment of organizations or by the internal one, and occasionally by a combination of the two of them simultaneously. Major events in the general environment, which appear unexpectedly as "random shocks," affect the life chances of organizations. The so-called "task environment," in contrast, affects organizational failure by gradual processes of niche erosion, such as shrinking markets or diminishing resources.

The structural configuration of organizations, their socioeconomic composition, cultural values, and behavioral patterns constitute their internal environment. Organizations' structures differ one from the others in their levels of centralization, formalization, and functional differentiation. The socioeconomic dimension of an organization is defined by parameters reflecting its social strength, in terms of quantity and quality of the human resource. It also indicates the economic vigor of organizations. The cultural dimension of organizations represents basic assumptions, main values, and social norms. Organizational behavior refers primarily to the ways in which executives and managers actually lead their organizations to the attainment of their goals. This dimension indicates the management's strategic choices, policymaking, leadership style, and its ability to cope with crises.

The underlying assumption of this volume is that organizations of all kinds are essentially one kind of open system. As such, they maintain ongoing reciprocal exchange relationships with their external environments, without which they have no chance of survival. Accordingly, it is plausible to compare organizations to biotic systems in general and to human beings in particular. To avoid misunderstanding, it is emphasized throughout this book that organizations are by no means natural systems. However, solely for the sake of the arguments presented here, it is worth considering them as if they were so. This use of this analogy facilitates the analytic task, as it makes it possible to deal with abstract phenomena in the realm of organizations in more concrete terms.

Following this line of thought, the key-concept used throughout this book is *pathology*. This concept serves here as a metaphor for analyzing life threatening problems in organizations and their effects on an organization's chances of survival. The notion of organizational pathology, then, becomes a useful tool for addressing a variety of issues. From this viewpoint, inherent inefficiencies, stagnating inertia, loss of direction, and members' counter-productive behaviors represent a few examples of organizational pathologies. The presence of these and other essentially abnormal patterns jeopardizes the life chances of organizations, leading to their eventual death. Once a certain pattern can be identified as pathological, it is possible to trace its pathogenesis, namely, the cause, development, and effects of such a disease.

This volume deals with three common pathologies, of a devastating nature, in the world of organizations. The first one, organizational politics, refers to ongoing power struggles in organizations, in which interest groups apply various kinds of political tactics against each other for the purpose of maximizing their benefits at the expense of the organization at large. Such battles inevitably weaken the organization, divide it into contesting components, drain its resources, and drag it to a state of paralysis. The second pathology, organizational corruption, reflects repeated misconduct, such as fraud or theft, undertaken by the organization's members, due to greed. Corruption is likely to start at the top of the hierarchy and spread downwards to the lower echelons as well. The third pathology, corporate crime, consists of various kinds of illegal activities, deliberately committed to mislead shareholders, governmental authorities, and the public at large. Corporate crime is intended to benefit the organization and improve its competitive position by means of concealed criminal acts, false reports, and fraudulent manipulations.

These major misconducts, and other ones of this kind, resemble life-threatening illnesses that will eventually push the "sick organization" to its death. They constitute deviant conducts that cannot be "brushed under the organization's carpet" for long. Eventually, they are most likely to be unveiled to the public in one way or another. In such cases, the focal organizations lose two of their most precious assets: their legitimacy and integrity. Therefore, their chances of survival become rather doubtful. Their death might take the form of an abrupt collapse or a long and painful process of shrinkage. Using the medical analogy, the differences between the outcomes of such pathologies is equivalent to the difference between death due to stroke and death due to a prolonged and agonizing fatal disease.

The so-called process of "organizational decline" is typical of the latter, representing a descending road that ends in organizational death. Declining organizations undergo diminution of their resources, gradual loss of vigor, and a continual loss of adaptability to changing environments. Consequently, they face an increasing probability of extinction as they continue along their course of decline. However, organizations undergoing decline processes do not necessarily die, at least not in the short-run. In quite a few cases, an organization's top management was able to make appropriate decisions and apply corrective measures, which led their organization to turn around and emerge from the process of decline. In fact, some organizations experience several cycles of decline and incline during their lifetime, rising again like the Phoenix Syndrome. Similar to terminal illnesses, in which the quality of medical treatment determines the chances of remission, the quality of the management's handling of a decline determines the likelihood of turnaround.

Organizations of all types—young and old, small and large, private and public—are ever at risk of encountering crises. According to the life-cycle perspective, organizations engage in expected crises of one kind or another at every developmental stage of life. Each crisis needs to be resolved in order for the organization to grow into the next life stage. A failure to cope with such a developmental crisis leads the organization to a state of fixation; in some cases, fixated organizations are likely to decline all the way down to a point of termination. Fixated organizations are unable to adapt to either their external or their internal environments. They actually stick to the conducts of earlier life stages of development. Following the psychological analogy, at least some of the fixated organizations display patterns of behavior that are abnormal at their age and size, that is, unsuitable to their level of development.

Contrary to the assumption that crises occur unexpectedly, there are early warning signals indicating that a crisis is on the way. Evidently, there are cases in which top management did not take such signals seriously and even tended to ignore them altogether. By estranging themselves, executives may go on with "business as usual," and refrain from applying the requisite precautionary measures. Thus, denial of forthcoming crises is neither a rational decision nor a calculated risk; rather, it is hiding ones' head in the sand.

Under such circumstances, unprepared organizations "suddenly" encounter crises that may be potentially life threatening to them. Indeed, in this situation, quite a few organizations do not survive the crisis. Those that do survive are likely to be crisis prone organizations, liable to undergo recurrent crises during their lifetime. In contrast, attentive and well-prepared organizations are those that employ the appropriate tools to cope with crises—before, during, and after they actually occur. These tools are usually packaged in crisis management plans.

Plenty of organizations everywhere fail to produce their goods and services efficiently and to deliver orders to their clientele as expected. From an economic point of view, failing organizations are likely to die, since their inefficiencies do not enable them to maintain themselves. However, many of them do survive for shorter or longer periods. This anomaly is an outcome of the interest of certain stakeholders to keep such organizations operative despite poor performance. The reasons for such preferences are usually selfish ones. In short, the benefit of maintaining a failing organization is greater than the cost of doing so. No wonder, then, that interest groups such as labor unions, political parties, customers, and suppliers, exert their power to protect certain failing organizations from dissolution. Consequently, some survive the crisis but continue to operate as permanently failing organizations.

However, the survival of any kind of failing organization should not be considered a necessarily favorable development, as the organization is destined to suffer a long and painful process until its inevitable demise. This process resembles dying processes of human beings who suffer from terminal illnesses. Yet, unlike the latter, dying organizations need to be disbanded prior to their final closure. This is a rather complicated and stressful process consisting of several stages, each of which requires different skills. Disbandment requires careful and systematic handling, to allow members and other stakeholders to undergo the process of departure from the dying organization and to accept its final closure.

At last, the idea of organizational pathology may enable students of organizations to broaden their understanding of them and to examine them in more realistic outlook. Practitioners are most likely to benefit as well from the notion of organizational pathology in their ongoing effort to improve the life chances of organizations, prevent their failure, and avoid their demise.

References

Adizes, I. 1979. "Organizational Passages—Diagnosing and Treating Life Cycle Problems of Organizations." *Organizational Dynamics* 8:3-25.

Adizes, I. 1988. *Corporate Life Cycle*. Englewood Cliffs, NJ: Prentice Hall.

Albrecht, S. 2006. "Organizational Politics: Affective Reactions, Cognitive Assessments and Their Influence on Organizational Commitment and Cynicism toward Change." Pp. 230-252 in *Handbook of Organizational Politics*, edited by E. Vigoda-Gadot and A. Drory. Cheltenham, UK: Edward Elgar.

Aldrich, H. E. 1979. *Organizations and environments*. Horward Englewood Cliffs, NJ: Prentice-Hall.

Aldrich, H. E. 1980. *Organizations and Environments*. Englewood Cliffs, NJ: Prentice-Hall.

Aldrich, H. E. and E. R. Auster. 1986. "Even Dwarfs Started Small: Liabilities of Age and Size and Their Strategic Implications." Pp. 165-198 in *Research in Organizational Behavior*, Vol. 8, edited by B. M. Staw and L. L. Cummings, Greenwich, CT: JAI Press.

Aldrich, H. A. and S. Mueller. 1982. "The Evaluation of Organizational Forms: Technology, Coordination, and Control." Pp: 33-87 in *Research in Organizational behavior*, Vol. 4, edited by B.M. Staw and L.L. Cummings, Greenwich, CT: JAI Press.

Altman, E. I. 1983. *Corporate Financial Distress: A Complete Guide to Predicting, Avoiding, and Dealing with Bankruptcy*. New York: Wiley.

Andersen, Arthur. 2008. "Accounting Scandals." (http//en.wikipedia.org/(Wiki/Arthur Andersen).

Anheier, H. K. (Ed.). 1999. *When Things Go Wrong: Organizational Breakdowns and Failures*. London: Sage.

Anheier, H. K. and L. Moulton. 1999. "Studying Organizational Failures." Pp. 273-290 in W*hen Things Go Wrong: Organizational Breakdowns Failures*, edited by H. K. Anheier. London: Sage.

Argenti, J. 1976. *Corporate Collapse: The Causes and Symptoms*. London: McGraw-Hill.

Argyris, C. 1982. *Reasoning, Learning and Action: Individual and Organizational*. San Francisco: Jossey-Bass.

Ashforth, B. E., Gioia, D. A., Robinson, S. L., and L. K. Trevino. 2008. "Special Topic Forum on Corruption in Organizations: Re-viewing Organizational Corruption." *Academy of Management Review* 33:670-684.

Bacharach, S., and E.J. Lawler. 1980. Power and Politics in Organizations. San Francisco: Jossey-Bass.

Bakan, J. 2004. *The Corporation: The Pathological Pursuit of Profit and Power.* New York: The Free Press.

Barker, V. L. and I. M. Duhaime. 1997. "Strategic Change in the Turnaround Process: Theory and Empirical Evidence." *Strategic Management Journal* 18:13-38.

Barlow, D. H. and V. Durant. 2002. *Abnormal Psychology*. 3rd ed. Belmont, CA: Wadsworth.

Barnett, W. P. and G. R. Carroll. 1987. "Competition and Mutualism among Early Telephone Companies." *Administrative Science Quarterly* 32:400-421.

Barron, D. N., West, E., and M. T. Hannan. 1994. "A Time to Grow and a Time to Die: Growth and Mortality of Credit Unions in New York City 1914-1990." *American Journal of Sociology* 100:381-421.

Baum, J. A. C. and J. Singh. 1994. "Organizational Niches and the Dynamics of Organizational Mortality." *American Journal of Sociology* 100:346-380.

Baum, J. A. C. and C. Oliver. 1991. "Institutional Linkages and Organizational Mortality." *Administrative Science Quarterly* 36:381-421.

Bergman, P. and R. Wigbald. 1999. "Workers' Last Performance: Why Some Factories Show their Best Results during Countdown." *Economic and Industrial Democracy* 20:343-368.

Bibeault, D. B. 1982. *Corporate Turnaround: How Managers Turn Losers into Winners*. New York: McGraw-Hill.

Blake, E. A., Gioia, D. A., Robinson, S. L. and L. K. Trevino. 2008. "Reviewing Organizational Corruption." *Academy of Management Review* 33:670-684.

Blau, P. M. 1964. *Exchange and Power in Social Life*. New York: Wiley.

Block, Z. and I. C. MacMillan. 1985. "Milestones for Successful Venture Planning." *Harvard Business Review* 63:184-196.

Booth, S. A. 1993. *Crisis Management Strategy: Competition in Modern Enterprises*. London: Routledge.

Box, S. 1983. *Power, Crime and Mystification*. London: Tavistock.

Braithewaite, J. 1989a. *Crime, Shame and Reintegration*. Sydney: Cambridge University Press.

Braithewaite, J. 1989b. "Criminological Theory and Organizational Crime." *Justice Quarterly* 6:333-358.

Bozeman, B. and E. A. Slusher. 1979. "Scarcity and Environmental Stress in Public Organizations." *Administration and Society* 11:335-355.

Braithwaite, J. 1989. *Crime, Shame, and Integration*. Cambridge: Cambridge University Press.

Brüderl, J. K., and R. Schüssler. 1990. "Organizational Mortality: The Liability of Newness and Adolescence." *Administrative Science Quarterly* 35:530-542.

Bryce, R. 2003. *Pipe Dream: Greed, Ego, and the Death of Enron*. New York: Public Affairs.

Burke, R. H. and L. Cooper (Eds.). 2000. *The organization in Crisis: Downsizing, Restructuring, and Privatization*. Malden, MA: Blackwell.

Cameron, K. S., Kim, M. U., and D.A. Whetten. 1987. "Organizational Effects of Decline and Turbulence." *Administrative Science Quarterly* 32:222- 240.

Cameron, K. S. and R. Miles. 1982. *Coffin Nails and Corporate Strategies*. Englewood Cliffs, NJ: Prentice-Hall.

Cameron, K. S., Sutton, R. I., and D. Whetten (Eds.). 1988. *Readings in Organizational Decline: Frameworks, Research, and Prescriptions*. Cambridge, MA: Ballinger.

Cameron, K. S. and D. A. Whetten. 1983. *Organizational Effectiveness: A Comparison of Multiple Models*. NY: Academic Press.

Cameron, K. S., Whetten, D. A., and M. U. Kim. 1987. "Organizational Dysfunctions of Decline." *Academy of Management Journal* 30:16-138.

Carmeli, A. and J. Shaubroeck. 2008. "Organizational Crisis-Preparedness: The Importance of Learning from Failure." *Long Range Planning* 41:177-196.

Carroll, G. R. 1984. "Organizational Ecology." *Annual Review of Sociology* 10:71-93.

Carroll, G. R. 1985. "Concentration and Specialization: Dynamics of Niche Width in Populations of Organizations." *American Journal of Sociology* 90:1262-1283.

Carroll, G. R. 1987. *Publish and Perish*. Greenwich, CT: JAI Press.

Carroll, G. and J. Delacroix. 1982. "Organizational Mortality in the Newspaper Industries in Argentina and Ireland: An Ecological Approach." *Administrative Science Quarterly* 27:169-198.

Carroll, G. R. and M. T. Hannan. 2000. *The Demography of Corporations and Industries*. Princeton, NJ: Princeton University Press.

Carroll, G. R. and Y. P. Huo. 1986. "Organizational Task and Institutional Environments in Ecological Perspective: Findings from the Local Newspaper Industry." *American Journal of Sociology* 91:838-873.

Chandler, A. D. 1962. *Strategy and Structure*. Cambridge, MA: MIT Press.

Chong, K. S. 2004. "Six Steps to Better Crisis Management." *Journal of Business Strategy* 25:43-46.

Chowdhury, S. D. 2002. "Turnarounds: A Stage Theory Perspective." *Canadian Journal of Administrative Sciences* 19:249-266.

Churchill, N. C. and V. L. Lewis. 1983. "The Five Stages of Small Business Growth." *Harvard Business Review* 61:30-50.

Clegg, S. R., Courpasson, D., and N. Phillips. 2006. *Power and Organizations*. London: Sage Publications.

Clinard, M. B. and P. M. Yeager. 2006. *Corporate Crime*. New Brunswick (USA) and London (U.K.): Transaction Publishers.

Cruver, B. 2002. *Anatomy of Greed: The Unshredded Truth from Enron Insider.* New York: Carroll and Graf Publishers.

Cunningham, J. B. 1997. "Feelings and Interpretations during Organization Death." *Journal of Organizational Change Management* 10:471-90.

Curram, S. P. and J. Mingers. 1994. "Neural Networks, Decision Tree: Induction and Discriminate Analysis: An Empirical Comparison." *Journal of Operational Research Society* 45:440-450.

Cyert, R. M. and J. G. March. 1963. *A Behavioral Theory of the Firm*. Englewood Cliffs, NJ: Prentice-Hall.

Daft, R. L. 2004. *Organization Theory and Design*. (7ed.), Cincinnati, Ohio: South-Western.

D'Aveni, R. A. 1989. "Dependability and Organizational Bankruptcy: An Application of Agency and Prospect Theory." *Management Science* 35:1120-1138.

D'Aveni, R. A. and Y. C. MacMillan. 1990. "Crisis and the Content of the Focus of Managerial Communications: A Study of Top Managers in Surviving and Failing Firms." *Administrative Science Quarterly* 35, 4:634-657.

DiMaggio, P. 1989. "Forward." P. 9 in *Permanently Failing Organizations,* by M. W. Meyer and L. G. Zucker. Newbury Park, CA: Sage.

Dimitras, A. I., Zanakis, S. H., and C. Zopounidis. 1996. "A Survey of Business Failure with an Emphasis on Prediction Method and Industrial Applications." *European Journal of Operational Research* 90:487–513.

Dobrev, S. D. and G. R. Carroll. 2003. "Size (and Competition) among Organizations: Modeling Scale-Based Selection among Automobile Producers in Four Major Countries, 1885-1981." *Strategic Management Journal* 24:541 558.

Du, L., and T. L. Tang. 2005. "Measurement of Invariance Across Gender and Major: The Love of Money among University Students in the Republic of China." *Journal of Business Ethics* 59:281-293.

Edelhertz, H. 1970. *The Nature, Impact, and Prosecution of White-collar Crime*. Washington, D.C.: U.S. Government Printing Office.

Edelhertz, H. 1983. "White-Collar and Professional Crime: The Challenge of the 1980s." *American Behavioral Scientists* 27:109-128.

Edwards, B. and S. Marullo. 1995. "Organizational Mortality in Declining Social Movements: The Demise of Peace Movement Organizations in the End of the Cold War Era." *American Sociological Review* 60:908-927.

Elusbbaugh, S., Fildes, R. and M. B. Rose. 1995. "Preparation for Crisis Management: A Proposed Model and Empirical Evidence." *Journal of Contingencies and Crisis Management* 12: 112-127.

Emery, F. E. and E. L. Trist. 1965. "The Casual Texture of Organizational Environments." *Human Relations* 18:21-32.

Etzioni, A. 1984. *Capital Corruption: The New Attack on American Democracy.* New York: Harcourt, Brace Jovanovich Publishers.

Fichman, M. and D. A. Levinthal. 1991. "Honeymoons and the Liability of Adolescence: A New Perspective on Duration Dependence in Social and Organizational Relationships." *The Academy of Management Review* 16:442-468.

Fink, S. L., Beak, J. and K. Taddeo. 1971. "Organizational Crisis and Change." *Journal of Applied Behavioral Science* 7:15-37.

Fleming, P. and A. Spicer. 2007. *Contesting the Corporation: Struggle, Power and Resistance in Organizations.* Cambridge: Cambridge University Press.

Forrester, J. W. 1971. *Principles of systems.* Cambridge, MA: Wright-Allen.

Freeman, J. 1982. "Organizational Life-Cycles and Natural Selection Processes." *Research in Organizational Behavior* 4:1-32.

Freeman, J., Carroll G. R., and M. T. Hannan. 1983. "The Liability of Newness: Age Dependence in Organizational Death Rates." *American Sociological Review* 48:692-710.

Fritz, K. P. and M. Holweg. 2003. "Exploring Scale: The Advantage of Thinking Small." MIT *Sloan Management Review (Winter)* 33-39.

Gabor, T. 1994. *Everybody Does It: Crime by the Public.* Toronto: University of Toronto Press.

Galbraith, J. 1982. "The Stages of Growth." *Journal of Business Strategy* 3:70-79.

Ginter, P. M., Duncan, J. W., Swayne, L. E., & A. G. Shelfer, Jr. 1992. "When Merger Means Death: Organizational Euthanasia and Strategic Choice." *Organizational Dynamics*, 20:3-21.

Greenberg, J. 1993. "Stealing in the Name of Justice: Informational and Interpersonal Moderators of Theft Reactions to Underpayment Inequity." *Organizational Behavior and Human Decisions Processes* 54:81-103.

Greenhalgh, L. 1983. "Organizational Decline." Pp. 231-276 in *Research in the Sociology of Organizations*, Vol. 2, edited by S. Bacharach.

Greiner, L. E. 1972. "Evolution and Revolution as Organizations Grow." *Harvard Business Review* 50:37-46.

Greiner, L. E. 1998. "Evolution and Revolution as Organizations Grow." *Harvard Business Review* May-June: 55-67.

Gouldner, A. W. (Ed.) 1965. *Studies in Leadership: Leadership and Democratic Action.* New York: Russell & Russell.

Gunn, H. and S. Chen. 2006. "A Micro-political Perspective of Strategic Management." Pp. 209-229 in *Handbook of Organizational Politics*, edited by E. Vigoda-Gadot and A. Drory. Cheltenham: Edward Edward Elgar.

Guy, M. E. 1989. *From Organizational Decline to Organizational Renewal:The Phoenix Syndrome.* New York: Quorum Books.

Halliday, T. C., Powell M. J., and M. W. Granfors. 1987. "Minimalist Organizations: Vital Events in State Bar Associations, 1870-1930." *American Sociological Review* 52:456-471.

Hambrick, D. C. and R. A. D'Aveni. 1988. "Large Corporate Failures as Downward Spirals." *Administrative science quarterly* 33:1-23.

Hambrick, D. C. and S. Schecter. 1983. "Turnaround Strategies for Mature Industrial-Product Business Units." *Academy of Management Journal* 26:231-248.

Hamilton, E. A. 2006. "An Exploration of the Relationship between Loss of Legitimacy and the Sudden Death of Organizations." *Group and Organization Management* 31:327-358.

Hanks, S. H. 1990. "An Empirical Examination of the Organization Life-Cycle High-Technology Organizations." Ph.D. Dissertation, University of Utah, *Business Review* 50:37-46.

Hanks, S. H., Watson, C. J., Jansen, E. and G. N. Chandler. 1993. "Tightening the Life-Cycle Construct: A Taxonomic Study of Growth Stage Configurations in High-Technology Organizations." *Entrepreneurship Theory and Practice* 17:5-29.

Hannan, M. T. 1989."Competitive and Institutional Processes in Organizational Ecology." Pp. 388-402 in *Sociological Theories in Progress: New Formulations,* edited by J. Berger, M. Zelditch, Jr. and B. Anderson. Newbury Park, CA: Sage Publications.

Hannan, M. T. 1992. *The Dynamics of Organizational Populations.* New York: Oxford University Press.

Hannan, M. T. 1998. "Rethinking Age Dependence in Organizational Mortality: Logical Formulations." *American Journal of Sociology* 104:126-164.

Hannan, M. T., and J. Freeman. 1984. "Structural Inertia and Organizational Change." *American Sociological Review* 49:149-164.

Hannan, M. T. and J. Freeman. 1989. *Organizational Ecology.* Cambridge, MA: Harvard Business Press.

Hannan, M. T., Carroll, G. R., and L. Pólos. 2003. "The Organizational Niche." *Sociological Theory* 21:309-340.

Hardy, C. and S. Clegg. 1996. "Some Dare Call it Power." Pp. 622-641 in *Handbook of Organization Studies,* edited by S.R. Clegg, C. Hardy, and W. R. Nord. London: Sage Publications.

Heywood, P. (Ed.). 1997. *Political Corruption.* Oxford, UK: Blackwell Publishers.

Hirschman, A. O. 1970. *Responses to Decline in Firms, Organizations, and States.* Cambridge, MA: Harvard University Press.

Hofer, C. W. 1980. "Turnaround Strategies." *Journal of Business Strategy* 1:19-31.

Huff, A. S. and J. O. Huff. 2000. *When Firms Change Direction.* Oxford, UK: Oxford University Press.

Hurst, D. K. 1995. *Crisis and Renewal: Meeting the challenge of Organizational Change.* Boston, MA: Harvard University Press.

Jas, P. and C. Skelcher. 2005. "Performance Decline and Turnaround in Public Organizations: A Theoretical and Empirical Analysis." *British Journal of Management* 16:195-210.

Jones, K. E., 2002. "Bankruptcy Prediction." (http://www.solvency.com).

Kanter-Moss, R. 2006. *Confidence: How Winning Streaks and Losing Streaks Begin and End.* New York: Three Rivers Press.

Katz, D. and R. L. Kahn. 1978. *The Social Psychology of Organizations.* 2nd edition, New York: Wiley.

Kazanjian, R. K. 1988. "Relationship of Dominant Problems to Stage of Growth Technology-Based New Ventures." *Academy of Management Journal* 31:257-279.

Kazanjian, R. and R. Drazin. 1989. "An Empirical Test of a Stage of Growth Progression Model." *Management Science* 35:1489-1503.

Kets de Vries, M. F. D. and D. Miller. 1984a. *The Neurotic Organization.* San Francisco: Jossey-Bass.

Kets de Vries, M. F. D. and D. Miller. 1984b. "Neurotic Style and Organization Pathology." *Strategic Management Journal* 5:35-55.

Kimberly, J. R. 1976. "Organizational Size and the Structuralist Perspective: A Review, Critique, and Proposal." *Administrative Science Quarterly* 32:571-597.

King, J. C. and A. W. Wicker. 1988. "The Population Demography of Organizations: An Application in Retail and Service Establishments." Forty-Eight Annual Meeting of the Academy of Management, Anaheim, CA (Best Papers Proceedings).

Koberg, C. S. 1987. "Resource Scarcity, Environmental Uncertainty, and Adaptive Organizational Behavior." *Academy of Management Journal* 30:798-807.

Kumar, P. R. and V. Ravi. 2007. "Bankruptcy Prediction in Banks and Firms via Statistical and Intelligent Techniques—A Review." *European Journal of Operational Research* 1:1-28.

Lamberg, J. A. and K. P Pajunen. 2005. "Beyond the Metaphor: The Morphology of Organizational Decline and Turnaround." *Human Relations* 58:947-980.

Lange, D. 2008. "A Multidimensional conceptualization of Organizational Corruption Control." *Academy of Management Review* 33:710-729.

Lawler, E. E. 1997. "Rethinking Organization Size." *Organizational Dynamics*, 26:24-35.

Levine, C. H. 1978. "Organizational Decline and Cutback Management." *Public Administration Review* 38: 316-325.

Levine, D. P. 2005. "The Corrupt Organization." *Human Relations* 58:723-740.

Levinthal, D. A. 1991. "Random Walks and Organizational Mortality." *Administrative Science Quarterly* 36:397-421.

Levinthal, D. A. 1997. "Adaptation on Rugged Landscapes." *Management Science* 43:934-950.

Lindenstrauss, M. 2007. *State Comptroller Annual Report,* Vol. 58A. Jerusalem: State of Israel (Hebrew).

Longenecker, C. O., Simonetti, J. L., & T. W. Sharskey. 1999. "Why Organizations Fail: The View from the Front-line." *Management Decision,* 37: 03-513.

McKinley, W. 1984. "Organizational Decline and Innovation in Manufacturing." Pp. 147-159 in *Strategic Management of Industrial R & D.* Edited by B. Bozerman, M. Crow and A. Link. Lexington, MA: Lexington Books.

McKinley, W. 1993. "Organizational Decline and Adaptation." *Organization Science* 4:1-9.

Meyer, M. W. and L. G. Zucker. 1989. *Permanently Failing Organizations.* Newbury Park, CA: Sage Publications.

Mellahi, K. P. and A. Wilkinson. 2004. "Organizational Failure: A Critique of Recent Research and a Proposed Integrative Framework." *International Journal of Management Review* 5-6:21-41.

Miles, R. H. and K. S. Cameron. 1982. *Coffin Nails and Corporate Strategies.* Englewood Cliffs, NJ: Prentice-Hall.

Miller, D. 1977. "Common Syndromes of Business Failures." *Business Horizons* 20:43-53.

Miller, D. 1992. "The Icarus Paradox: How Exceptional Companies Bring about Their Own Downfall." *Business Horizons* 35: 24-35.

Miller, D. and P. H. Friesen. 1984. "A Longitudinal Study of the Corporate Life Cycle." *Management Science* 30:1161-1183.

Miller, J. G. and J. L. Miller. 1991. "A Living System Analysis of Organizational Pathology." *Behavioral Science* 36:239-251.

Mintzberg, H. 1983. *Power in and Around Organizations.* Englewood Cliffs, NJ: Prentice-Hall.

Mitchell, T. R., and A. Mickel. 1999. "The Meaning of Money: An Individual Difference Perspective." *Academy of Management Review* 24:568-578.

Mossman, Ch. E., Bell, G. G., Swartz, L. M., and H. Turtle. 1998. "An Empirical Comparison of Bankruptcy Models." *The Financial Review* 33:35-54.

Ohlson, J.A. 1980. "Financial Rations and the Probabilistic Prediction of Bankruptcy." *Journal of Accounting Research* 18:109–131.

Ooghe, H., Spaenjers, C., and P. Vandermoere. 2005. "Business Failure Prediction: Simple-Intuitive Models Versus Statistical Models." Vlerick Leuven Gent Working Paper 2005/22.

Ormerod, P. 2006. *Why Most Things Fail: Evolution, Extinction and Economics.* London: Faber and Faber.

Orton, D. J., and K. E., Weick. 1990. "Loosley Coupled Systems: A Reconceptualization." *Academy of Mangement Review* 15:203-233.

Park, S. H. and M. V. Russo. 1996. "When Competition Eclipses Cooperation: An Event History Analysis of Joint Ventures Failure." *Management Science* 42:875-890.

Parker-Oliver, D. 1999-2000. "The Social Construction of the "Dying Role" and the Hospice Drama." *Omega-Journal of Death and Dying* 40:493-512.

Paton, R. and J. Mordaunt. 2004. "What's Different about Public and Non-Profit Turnarounds?" *Public Money and Management* 24:209-216.

Pearce, F. and L. Snider (Eds.). 1995. *Corporate Crime: Contemporary Debates.* Toronto: University of Toronto Press.

Pearce, J. A. and K. Robbins. 1993. "Toward Improved Theory and Research on Business Turnaround." *Journal of Management* 19:613-636.

Pearson, C. and I. Mitroff. 1993. "From Crisis-Prone to Crisis-Prepared: A Framework for Crisis Management." *Academy of Management Executive* 7:48-59.

Pfarrer, M. D., Decelles, K. A., Smith, K. G. and M. S. Taylor. 2008. "After the Fall: Reintegrating the Corrupt Organization." *Academy of Management Review* 33:730-749.

Pfeffer, J. 1981. *Power in Organization.* Marshfield, MA: Pitman.

Pinto, J., Leana, C. R. and F. K. Pil. 2008. "Corrupt Organizations or Organizations of Corrupt Individuals? Two Types of Organization-Level Corruption." *Academy of Management Review* 33:785-709.

Porta, della, D. and A. Vannuci. 1999. *Corrupt Exchanges: Actors, Resources, and Mechanisms of Political Corruption.* New York: Aldine de Gruyter.

Porta, della, D. and A. Vannuci.1997. "The 'Perverse Effects' of Political Corruption". Pp. 100-122 in *Political Corruption,* edited by P. Heywood. Oxford: Blackwell Publishers.

Quinn, R. E. and K. S. Cameron. 1983. "Organizational Life Cycle and Shifting Criteria of Effectiveness: Some Preliminary Evidence." *Management Science* 29:33-51.

Ray, M. and A. Rinzler (Eds.). 1993. *The New Paradigm in Business: Emerging Strategies for Leadership and Organizational Change.* New York: Putnam Sons.

Reber, A .1987. *The Penguin Dictionary of Psychology.* London: Penguin Books.

Richardson, B. 1995. "Paradox Management for Crisis Avoidance." *Management Decision* 33: 5-18.

Richardson, B., Nwanko, S., and S. Richardson. 1994. "Understanding the Causes of Business Failure Crises." *Management Decision* 32:9-22.

Richardson, F. C. and G. I. Manaster. 1992. "Greed, Psychopathology, and Social Interest." *Individual Psychology* 48:261-276.

Rivlin, A. M. 2003. "Greed, Ethics, and Public Policy." *Public Integrity* 5:347-354.

Rose-Ackerman, S. 1999. *Corruption and Government: Causes, Consequences, and Reform.* New York: Cambridge University Press.

Rosenblatt, Z. and B. Mannheim. 1996. "Organization Response to Decline in the Israeli Electronics Industry." *Organization Studies* 17:953-984.

Samuel, Y. and S. Heilbrunn, 2001. "Entrepreneurship in the Kibbutz Setting: Towards a Classification of New Business Ventures." *Journal of Rural Corporation* 29:47-62.

Samuel, Y. and I. Harpaz (Eds.). 2004. *Work and Organizations in Israel*. Schnitzer Studies in Israeli Society, Vol. 11. New Brunswick, NJ & London: Transaction Publishers.

Samuel, Y. 2005. *The Political Agenda of Organizations*. New Brunswick, NJ & London: Transaction Publishers.

Scott, J. 1981. "The Probability of Bankruptcy." *Journal of Banking and Finance* 5:317-344.

Scott, W. R .1992. *Organizations: Rational, Natural, and Open Systems*. 3rd edition, Englewood Cliffs, NJ: Prentice-Hall.

Seeman, M. 1959. "On the Meaning of Alienation." *American Sociological Review* 24:783-791.

Seeman, M. 1975. "Alienation Studies." *Annual Review of Sociology* 1:91-123.

Sheaffer, Z., Richardson, B. and Z. Rosenblatt. 1998. "Early-Warning-Signals Management: A Lesson from the Barings Crisis." *Journal of Contingencies and Crisis Management* 6:1-22.

Sheppard, J. P. 1994. "Strategy and Bankruptcy: An Exploration into Organizational Death." *Journal of Management*, 20: 795-834.

Singh, J. V., R. House, and J. D. Tucker. 1986. "Organizational Change and Organizational Mortality." *Administrative Science Quarterly* 31:587-611.

Slapper, G. and S. Tombs. 1999. *Corporate Crime*. Essex, UK: Longman.

Staw, B. M., Sandelands, L. E. and J. E. Dutton. 1981. "Threat Rigidity Effects in Organizational Behavior: A Multilevel Analysis." *Administrative Science Quarterly* 26:501-524.

Stead, E. and V. Smallman. 1999. "Understanding Business Failure: Learning and Unlearning Lessons from Industrial Crises." *Journal of Contingencies and Crisis Management* 7:1-19.

Stinchcombe, A. L. 1965. "Social Structure and Organizations." Pp. 142-193 in *Handbook of Organizations*, edited by James G. March. Chicago: Rand McNally.

Suchman, M. C. 1995. "Mapping legitimacy: Strategic and Institutional Approaches." *Academy of Management Review* 20:571-610.

Sutherland, E. H. 1949. *White Collar Crime*. New York: Holt.

Sutton, R. I. 1983. "Managing Organizational Death." *Human Resource Management* 22:391-412.

Sutton, R. I. 1987. "The Process of Organizational Death: Disbanding and Reconnecting." *Administrative Science Quarterly* 32:542-569.

Sutton, R. I. 2005. "Organizational Decline and Death," Pp. 1 in *The Blackwell Encyclopedic Dictionary of Organizational Behavior*, edited by N. Nicholson. Cambridge, MA: Blackwell Publishers.

Tombs, S. 1995. "Corporate Crime and New Organizational Forms." Pp. 132-146 in *Corporate Crime: Contemporary Debates*, edited by F. Pierce and L. Snider. Toronto: University of Torornto Press.

Tushman, M. L. and E. Romanelli. 1985. "Organizational Evolution: A Metamporphosis Model of Convergence and Reorientation." *Research in Organizational Behavior* 7:171-222. JAI Press.

Vardi, Y. and E. Weitz. 2004. *Misbehavior in Organizations: Theory, Research, and Management*. Mahwah, NJ: Lawrence Warlbaum.

Van de Ven, A. H. 1980. "Early Planning, Implementation and Performance of New Organizations." Pp. 83-134 in *The Organizational Life Cycle*, edited by J. R. Kimberly, et al., San Francisco: Jossey-Bass.

Vigoda-Gadota, E. and A. Drory (Eds.). 2006. *Handbook of Organizational Politics.* Cheltenham, UK: Edgar Elgar.

Weitzel, W. and E. Jonsson. 1989. "Decline in Organizations: A Literature Integration and Extension." *Administrative Science Quarterly* 34:91-109.

Weitzel, W. and E. Jonsson. 1991. "Reversing the Downward Spiral: Lessons from W. T. Grant and Sears Roebuck." *Academy of Management Executive* 5:7-21.

Whetten, D. A. 1980. "Sources, Responses, and Effects of Organizational Decline" Pp. 342-374. In *The Organizational Life Cycle*, edited by J. R. Kimberly, et al., San Francisco: Jossey-Bass.

Whetten, D. A. 1980. "Organizational Decline: A Neglected Topic in Organizational Science." *Academy of Management Review* 5:577-588.

Whetten, D. A. 1987. "Organizational Growth and Decline Processes." *Annual Review of Sociology* 13:335-358.

Whetten, D. A. 1988. "Sources, Responses, and Effects of Organizational Decline." Chapter 8, Pp. 151-174 In *Readings in Organizational Decline,* edited by Cameron, Sutton, and Whetten. Cambridge, MA: Ballinger.

Wigbald, R. 1995. "Community Turnarounds in Declining Company Towns: A Restructuring Model." *The Journal of Socio-Economics* 24:463-475.

Wilcox, J. W. A. 1973. "A Prediction of Business Failure Using Accounting Data, Empirical Research in Accounting: Selected studies." *Journal of Accounting Research* 11:163–179.

Wiseman, R. M. and P. Bromiley. 1996. "Toward a Model of Risk in Declining Organizations: An Empirical Examination of Risk, Performance, and Decline." *Organization Science* 7:527-543.

van Witteloostuijn, A. 1998. "Bridging Behavioral and Economic Theories of Decline: Organizational Inertia, Strategic Competition, and Chronic Failure." *Management Science* 44:501-520.

Zammuto, R. F. and K. S. Cameron. 1985. "Environmental Decline and Organizational Response." *Research in Organizational Behavior* 7:223-262.

Zelditch, M. B. Jr., Berger, J. and B. P. Cohen. 1966. "Stability of Organizational Status Structures" Pp. 269-294. In *Sociological Theories in Progress,* Vol. 1, edited by J. Berger, M. Zelditch, Jr. and B. Anderson. Boston: Houghton Mifflin Company.

Index